Measurement Fundamentals and Systems

Dr. Patil Shriram B.

M.Sc. D.H.E. Ph.D

Associate professor,

Department of Physics,

S.S.V.P.S.L.K.Dr.P.R.Ghogrey Science College,

Deopur, Dhule

Maharashtra (India)

Published By:

OpenCrayons.com

Wordit Content Design & Editing Services Pvt Ltd.
Newbridge Business Centre, C38/39,
Parinee Crescenzo Building,
G Block,Bandra Kurla Complex, Bandra East,
Mumbai 400 051, India
T: +91 8080226699

Internationally published

ISBN: 978-93-86487-05-6

Preface

I am very happy to place this book *'Measurement Fundamentals and Systems'* in the hands of under graduate students, especially the students from North Maharashtra University, Jalgon (Maharashtra, India). Physics is probably the most applicable of the three pure sciences Biology, Chemistry and Physics. The study of physics is not meant to answer fundamental questions about our existence in this wonderful universe. In physics, scientists make observations, develop theories, experiment and revise their theories. Physics tells us how gravity behaves but does not speak to the origin of gravity's. Instrumentation is one of the active branches in physics. Instrumentation has become a very important subject as an interdisciplinary course in almost all universities. This book is intended as a standard text for the students studying for their under graduation and graduation. Instrumentation and electronic instrumentation is offered as separate paper in recent years in number of Universities. The content of the book is having been well arranged, Initial five chapters discusses the fundamentals of measurement system. In the last six chapters the measurement systems for different parameters has been discussed in brief with the necessary diagrams. Separate chapters are devoted to topics like generalized measurement system, transducers, Data acquisition system, input output devices etc. There is an additional chapter on the static and dynamic characteristics of measurement system. A reasonably wide coverage in sufficient depth has been attempted, *giving the importance to the basic principles, essential theory and experimental details necessary for understanding the nature, properties and applications of instrument. All efforts have been made to provide topics which are of great use to the readers.*

I am especially indebted to the kindness of our inspirational source Hon'ble Shri Rohidasji Patil (Ex Minister Maharashtra State) and Hon'ble Mrs. Latataie Rohidasji Patil. Special thanks to our Hon'ble management members, Principal Dr. D.A.Patil who has always afforded me facilities for my academic developments. The author is grateful to Prof. M.A.More for his constant support and encouragement. The author is thankful to his wife Surekha, son Dr. Rohan and daughter Dr. Shweta for rendering their assistance in the compilation and editing of the book. I am thankful to M/s Wordit Content Design and Editing services private (P) Limited Publishers, Mumbai, for their untiring efforts in bringing out the book with excellent printing and nice get up within the shortest possible time period.

In spite of great care, some misprints and omissions might have crept in. author will be grateful to readers who will point them out. Suggestions for the improvement of the book are most welcome.

Author

INDEX

1. Measurement fundamentals:

1.1. Introduction:

Instrumentation is one of the branch of physics and technology of measurement which serves sciences, medicine, engineering and number of all other branches. Measurement is the process of determining the amount, degree or capacity by comparison with the accepted standards of the system units being used and the instrument is a device which is used to determine the value or magnitude of a quantity or variable.

There are three basic functions of instrumentation,

1) Indication – To visualize the process or operation.
2) Recording – To observe and save the measurement reading in any form.
3) Controlling – To control the measurement and measurement process.

Whenever one has to use any instrument for the measurement, he should be thoroughly familiar with its operation. He should select an instrument which will provide the degree of accuracy required.

1.2: Characteristics of Instruments:

1.2.1: Performance Characteristics

The characteristics which show the performance of an instrument are the performance characteristics.

For example, accuracy, sensitivity linearity, precision, resolution etc. Taking into account the performance characteristics, the users should select the most suitable instrument for a specific measuring job.

There are two basic characteristics Static and Dynamic. The performance characteristics of the instruments are,

1. Accuracy:

The Accuracy is the degree of closeness to the true or desired value of measurement. The accuracy of the measurement is the approximation of the measurement to the actual values. When the number of significant figures increases the measurement becomes more and more accurate. For example, if the length or thickness is measured by meter scale it shows 4.2cm, while it shows 4.23 when it measured by vernier caliper and it will shows 4.234, when it measured with micrometer screw gage. If the numbers of readings are increased so that taking the mean value, the accuracy can be increased.

2. Resolution:

The resolution is the fineness to which an instrument can be read. The smallest change in a measurement variable to which an instrument will respond. For example, the resolution of analog stopwatch may be 1/10 second but the resolution of digital stopwatch will be 1/100 second.

3. Precision:

It is the ability of an instrument in measuring the quantity in a consistent manner. It is a measure of repeatability of the measurement. It can be indicated by its relative deviation and can be defined in terms of percentage, as the ratio of mean deviation to the mean value multiplied by 100. [1]

4. True value:

True value means the most probable or expected value of the measurement.

1.2.2: Dynamic Characteristics: Dynamic means measuring a varying process condition. The dynamic characteristics of an instrument are:

1. Speed of response: it is the rapidity or quickness which an instrument responds to change in the measure quantity.

2. Response time: The time required by an instrument to settle to its final steady position after the application of input.

3. Drift: When instrument does not reproduce the same reading at different times of measurement for the same input signal, it is said to have drift. If an instrument has perfect reproducibility, it is said to have no drift.

4. Measuring lag: An instrument doesn't immediately react to a change it is the delay in response of an instrument to a change in a measured quantity

5. Fidelity: It is the ability of the system or instrument to reproduce the output in the same form as input. For example, if the input to the system is a square wave, the

system is said to have 100% fidelity if the output also is a square wave.

6. Dynamic error: It is the difference between the true value of the quantity changing with time and the value indicated by the instrument if no static error is assume. The total dynamic error of the instrument is the combination of its fidelity and the time lag or phase difference between input and output devices. [2]

Resolution:

The smallest change in a measured value, the instrument detects. It is also known as sensitivity. Display resolution for screen sizes typically measured in inches and distinct pixel in each dimension that can be display. It is usually coated as width x height with the units in pixel for example 1024 x 768 means the width is 1024 pixels and height is 768 pixel. This example could normally be spoken as 1024 by 768. The term display resolution is usually used to mean the pixel dimension. The number of measurement it is given in pixel per inch. In analog measurement if the screen is 10 inch high then the horizontal resolution is measured across a sequence 10 inch wide This is typically states as lines horizontal resolution per picture height for example NTSC TV a display resolution486 lines of per picture height horizontal resolution which is equivalent to 648 total lines of actual picture information from left edge to right and its resolution is given right 648 x 486 in actual lines per information best per picture height a display – of 486 by 486.

Deadband:

A deadband sometimes is also called as neutral zone, is an area of a signal range or band where no action occurs. Deadband is the largest change in the physical variable to which the instrument doesn't respond. It means that, the region up to which the instrument doesn't respond for an input is called as the deadband. It means the system is dead for some time. Deadband is used in voltage regulator and other controllers; the purpose is to prevent oscillation or repeated activation deactivation cycles.

For example, in some substation there are regulators that keep the voltage within certain predetermined limits. There is a particular range of voltage in which no changes are made; for example, in the range of 112 to 118 volts deadband is 6 volts or 215 to 225 volts it is 10 volts.

Gear teeth with slope (black lash) exhibit deadband. There is no drive from the input to the output shaft in either direction, when the teeth are not meshed. [3]

Hysteresis:

When all the energy put into the stressed component when loaded is not recovered upon unloading. Hence the output of a measurement system will partly depend on its previous input signal and this is called as hysteresis. Hysteresis occurs in ferromagnetic materials and ferroelectric materials, in response to a varying driving force. When a ferromagnetic material undergoes magnetization with varying magnetic field intensity i.e. driving force, it traced out a loop called as a "hysteresis loop" as shown in following figure. When a ferromagnetic material is magnetized in one direction, the material follows a non linear magnetization curve, after a desired driving force the material magnetized to saturation by the alignment of domains. When the driving force i.e. magnetic field decreases to zero, it will not back to its initial position i.e. zero magnetization. It means, the ferromagnetic material retains some amount of magnetization. This residual magnetization is called as "Retentivity" or "residual magnetization". This property is useful for magnetic memory devices. To regain the zero magnetization, the driving magnetic field must be reversed and increased to a large value, this value in known as a coercive force or "Coercivity". When the applied magnetic field is again reversed i.e. from negative to Zero the material regain and retain the magnetization, it means it remember its history. The magnetization curve never retraced and is the property of the material called Hysteresis. The hysteresis is the property which is related to the magnetic domains of the material. When the field is applied to the magnetic material the magnetic domains get oriented and so that they take some energy to come back again. This is the property which is very useful as a magnetic memory. The plot of magnetization or flux density, M of the magnetic material as a function of magnetic field strength H, also called as magnetizing force (H is measure of applied field) is as shown in the following figure.

If the hysteresis loop is having large area, it means after removing the driving force, it retains a large fraction of the saturation magnetic field. This characteristic is desirable for permanent magnets and magnetic memory devices. [4, 5]

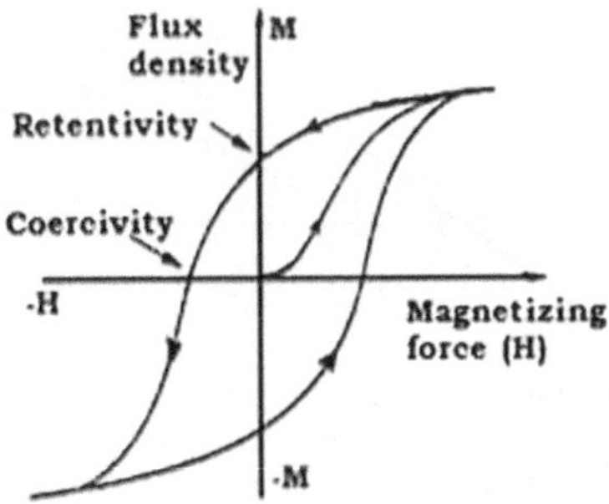

The narrow hysteresis loop means a small amount of energy dissipation in number of repetition of cycles. This characteristic is very useful for transformers to minimize the energy dissipation with the alternating field associated with AC electrical applications.

The hysteresis in general defined as the magnitude of error caused in the output for a given value of input when this value is approaches from opposite direction. The origin of this is backlash, elastic deformation, magnetic characteristic but it is mainly caused due to frictional effects. When there is a solid contact between dry surfaces friction comes into play. It is defined as the force or torque necessary to initiate the motion of the instrument. After friction dynamic friction comes into play and the input-output characteristic of the instrument takes the shape of closed curve known as hysteresis loop.

Drift:

The drift is defined as the variation of output for a given input caused due to change in sensitivity of the instrument to certain interfering inputs like temperature changes, component instability etc.

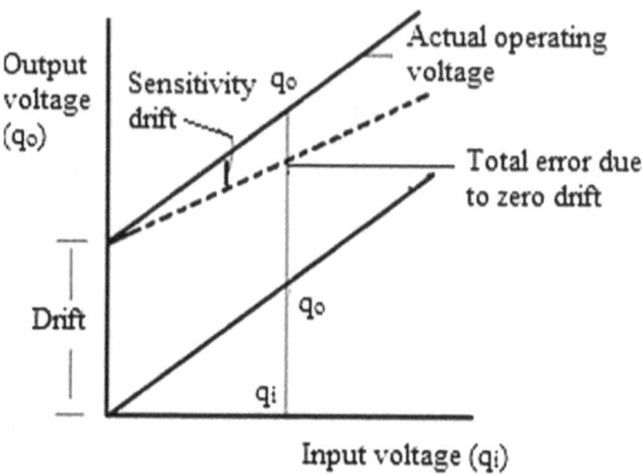

For example, a strain gauge bridge output without a compensating dummy strain gauge may indicate the input-output characteristic as shown in following figure. If the ambient (atmospheric) temperature changes after the calibration of instrument causes the changes in resistance of the strain gauge. This result that the bridge circuit becomes unbalanced and as a consequence there is zero strain which corresponds zero drift of the instrument. Further this resistance changes also affects the sensitivity of the instrument which result in the change of slope of the input-output characteristic (as in figure) Therefore the total error involved due to drift is a combined effect of the zero drift as well as the sensitivity drift.

Threshold:

It is a particular case of resolution. It is defined as the minimum value of input below which no output can be detected. Both threshold and resolution can either be specified as absolute quantities in terms of input units or a percentage of full scale deflection (F.S.D). Both threshold and resolution are not zero because of various factors like friction between moving parts, play (deviation) or looseness in joint, inertia of the moving parts, length of scale, size of the pointer, parallax effects etc.

Backlash:

The backlash sometimes is also called as lash or play. It is the maximum distance through which one part of the instrument may be moved without disturbing the other part. It is clearance between mating components sometime described as the amount of lost motion to Clarence or slackness when moment is reversed and contact is reestablished

For example, in a pair of gears, backlash is the amount of clearance between mated gear teeth. Theoretically a backlash should be zero but in actual practice some backlash must be allow to permits to prevent jamming.

Factor affecting the amount of backlash requires in a gear train includes error in profile peach, tooth thickness, helix angle and centre distance and run out. The greater the accuracy, smaller the backlash needed. Backlash is most commonly created by cutting the teeth deeper into the gears than the ideal depth. Backlash due to tooth thickness changes is typically measured along the pitch circle and is defined by $B_T = T_i - T_a$, where BT backlash due to tooth thickness modification Ti tooth thickness on the pitch circle for ideal gearing, Ta – actual tooth thickness.

Sensitivity:

The sensitivity of an instrument is its ability to detect small changes in the quantity that is being measured. The sensitive instrument can quickly detect small changes in the measurement. The instruments are more sensitive which are having smaller scale parts.

The Static sensitivity is also known as scale factor or gain. It can be calculated from the result of static calibration curve. It is defined as the ratio of the magnitude of response of the instrument (output signal) to the magnitude of the quantity being measured.

The sensitivity is represented by the slope of input - output curve, if the ordinates are represented on actual scales with linear calibration curve the sensitivity is constant as known as shown in following figure. However if the relationship between input and output is not linear the sensitivity varies with the input value.

Linearity:

A linear indicating scale is one of the most desirable features of any instrument therefore manufactures of instrument also attempt to design their instrument so that output is a linear function of the input however linearity is never completely achieved. The deviation from the ideal line termed as a linearity tolerance. In commercial instrument the maximum deviation from linearity is often specified in one of the following ways.

Independent of input:

If the deviation of the output of the instrument from the best fitting straight line draw through the calibration point doesn't vary with the input, it is said to be independent of input. Non-linearity in this case is specified in terms of higher value of the maximum deviation occurs on the positive and negative sides of the ideal line and this is expressed as percentage non-linearity (% nonlinearity) of full scale deflection.

Proportional to Input:

If the deviation of the output of the instrument from the ideal line vary with the input then linearity may referred as proportional to input. In such cases the non-linearity specified as a function of the input i.e. in this case the maximum deviation point on positive side is joining with the origin and their slope be determined. The Percentage (%) change in slope with respect to the ideal line is expressed as % of non-linearity.

Partially independent and partially proportional to input:

In certain cases the deviation of the output may not vary with the input. It may partly show output independent of input or show proportional variation for the rest of input. In this case the maximum deviation at the lower range is taken by specifying $\pm x$ % or $\pm y$% of the full scale deflection. In most commercial instruments linearity specification are equivalent to accuracy specification and either of them may be specified.

1.3: Classification of Instruments:

The instruments are broadly classified into two categories

1. Absolute

2. Secondary

Absolute: These devices give the magnitude of quantity under measurement in terms of physical constants of the instruments.

Secondary: These devices are so constructed that the quantity being measured can only be measured by observing the output indicated by the instruments. These instruments are calibrated by comparison with absolute instruments which has already being calibrated against absolute instruments. A voltmeter, a glass thermometer, a pressure gauge are some typical examples of secondary transducer.

The instruments can also be classified according to their operation and how and in which form they are used.

1.3.1: Self generating and power operated type instruments:

The self generating devices are active devices, which do not require any outside power to perform its function. For example the thermal expansion of the liquid is the motive power to glass in liquid thermometer and hence it is a self generated device. Similarly, the dial indicator is an active device, because all the energy required to operate the instrument is furnished by the system whose displacement is being measured. The exposure meter of camera, this is based on a photovoltaic effect. The bourdon tube for the measurement of pressure is also a self generating device. The Pitot tube, the device for the measurement of velocity of fluid is also a good example of active device.

On the other hand some instruments require power or source from outside to operate instruments, so that such devices are known as power operated or passive devices. For example, electricity, compressed air, hydraulic power are some auxiliary power sources used for the operation of the instruments. A differential transformer used is the measurement of displacement, force; pressure etc. is an example of power operated. The photoconductive transducer converts the light information into resistance change. The resistance thermometers and thermistors are the good examples of power operated type instruments.

1.3.2: Contacting and non-contacting type:

The name suggest their meaning, means when the instrument is in close proximity to the measurement, the device is called as a contacting type device. A clinical thermometer is one of the good examples of contacting type of instruments. When it is possible to measure the quantity very easy by keeping the measurement device very closely then the contacting type devices are used.

There are some measurements which cannot take by the observer with close proximity. Such measurement can be taken by the devices called as non-contacting type instruments. These devices measure the desired input even though they are not in close contact with the measuring media. An optical pyrometer is used to measure temperature of fire. The variable reluctance tachometer, used to measure the revolution per minute (R.P.M) of the rotating body. In this device, the teeth which are rotates made up of ferromagnetic material, causes variation of flux in the magnetic circuit due to changes in gear gaps, this in turn induces an electro motive force (emf) i.e. in the form of pulses. The output of instruments is fed to frequency counter from which the revolution per minute (R.P.M) of rotor can be determined.

1.3.3: Analog and digital instruments:

Secondary instruments work in two modes analog and digital. Signals that vary in a continuous fashion and take on infinity values in any given range are called analog signals, which produces these signal are called analog device. The numbers of meters like voltmeter, ammeter, speedometer, fuel meter works on the principle of moving coil etc are the examples of analog instruments. These are low cost devices and easy to maintain and also to repair. These devices don't give exact value of measurement.

The signal which vary in discrete steps and thus take up only finite different values in a given range are called digital signals and the devices which produce such signals are called digital devices. The main drawback of such devices is that they are unable to indicate the quantity which is a part of the step value of the instrument. These devices are having high sped, highly accurate and most important no man made errors are there to read or record the data.

For example, a digital resolution counter can't indicate say 0.65 of a resolution as it measures only in steps of one resolution

1.3.4: Deflection and null type instruments:

Deflection comes from "to deflect", in these types of instruments the pointer of the electrical measuring instrument deflects to measure the quantity. The quantity which value is to be measure can be measured by measuring the net deflection of the pointer from its initial position. In other words one can say a deflection type instruments means the physical effect created by the measuring quantity and which is associated to the measurand. The calibration of the deflection type instruments depends on the value of instrument constant. The display mechanism of a meter is often referred to as a moving coil; it means to move a pointer along a scale so that a measured value can be noted. To detect and display an electrical quantity, "meter" is a device which observer can used to accurately note in any form. The movement of a pointer on a scale indicates the particular value of that parameter. To measure the number of basic quantities like voltage, current, and resistance, meters are so designed will get the accurate measurement. Because of the inertial effect, the deflection type instruments are less accurate and are less sensitive than the null type of instruments. These instruments are more suitable under dynamic conditions.

The null type electrical measuring instruments, also called as zero type, tend to maintain the position of pointer stationary. By producing opposing effect, the position of the pointer makes stationary. The steps required for the operation of null type of instruments are first to calculate the value of unknown quantity, the Value of opposite effect should be known and the detector shows accurately the balance and the unbalance condition accurately. Null point type instruments are more sensitive

The difference between deflection and null type instruments can be easily understood by taking the example of platform scale and a two pan balance. In the two pan balance i.e. null type, the unknown quantity is placed in one of the pan while the weights are placed in the other pan still a balance condition i.e. zero can be achieved. The weights required to null the balance is the measurement of that quantity. In a platform scale, i.e. deflection type, the quantity which is to be measured placed on the platform of the scale and the relative displacement indicates the measurement of that quantity. [6, 7]

1.4: Functional elements of measurement System:

It is important to have a systematic organization and analysis of measurement system. Several measurement systems are in use today. Before measuring a physical quantity, it is necessary to understand the working of the measurement system used. Generalized measurement system is a system that is comprised of the typical elements of a measurement system. It helps to understand how a measurement system works.

A generalized measurement system consists of basic functional element and auxiliary elements. Basic functional elements are those which are integral part of all the instruments. The following figure depicts the measurement system along with the basic as well as auxiliary elements.

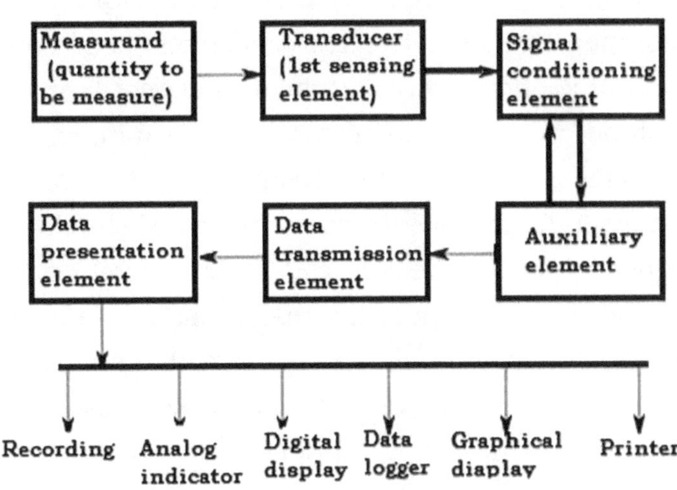

Figure: Functional elements of measurement system

The quantity which is to be measured is first sensed by the First Sensing Element or transducer. The transducer converts one form of energy into other. In measurement system the transducer senses the input and then converts it into desired output, which is fed to the signal processing unit. The numbers of transducers are available; one can choose the transducer as per their requirement. For example stethoscope of medical practitioner, the primary sensor is diaphragm, which is placed on the chest of the patient. The diaphragm senses the heart beats of the Patient and then it is forwarded and can be sense by the physician in the form of sound waves. The primary sensing element in an ammeter, is the coil which carrying the current to be measured.

The signal conditioning element also called as variable conversion element. Many times, the output of the Primary sensing element may not be suitable for the actual measurement system. The conversion element convert that output in such a way that the next element can easily understood in a particular form. For example, when an ammeter is used for the measurement of current, the output from the coil is current, so that there should place a magnet to get a deflection due to the current passing in the coil. It means, here the magnet acts as a variable conversion element, converting current into physical movement which is the deflection and by measuring the amount of deflection, amount of current can be measure. The conversion element is not compulsory to all the instruments and the original information should not change during the conversion process.

In addition to the basic blocks, the measurement system requires some auxiliary elements. Auxiliary means supplementary elements which may be in corporate in a particular system depending on the type of requirement, nature of measurement technique. To provide a built-in calibration facility, the Calibration element is used. The External power element to facilitate the working of one or more of the element like the transducer, signal conditioning element, data processing element etc. The Feedback element to control the variation of the physical quantity.

Many a times it is happen that, the level of the output from the Variable conversion element may not be enough for the next stage. For example, in case of an ammeter if the amount of current to be measured is so small, it may not be enough to cause any deflection in the magnet. At such a time a transformer can be used to increase the voltage to get enough deflection, in this case the transformer will be the Data Manipulation Element. Actually these both the Variable conversion element and the variable manipulation element are together called as Signal conditioning element since they help to obtain the signal in pure and acceptable form from highly distorted form.

Data processing element is an important element used in many measurement systems. It processes the data signal received from the variable manipulation element and produces suitable output. Data processing element may also be used to compare the measured value with a standard value to produce required output.

Data Transmission System is simply used for transmitting data from one element to another. It acts as a communication link between different elements of the measurement system. Some of the data transmission elements used are cables, wireless antennae, transducers, telemetry systems etc.

It is used to present the measured physical quantity in a. It receives processed signal from data processing element and presents the data in a human readable form. LED displays are most commonly used as data presentation elements in many measurement systems.

To present the measured physical quantity, say data in a human readable form or suitable form to the observer, the Data Presentation Element is used. There are number of data presentation elements, as per the requirement of the observer, the data presentation elements can be used. For example, in an ammeter the Pointer and the scale arrangement acts as the data presentation element. If the output data is to be monitored, a visual display like oscilloscopes can be use, if the data to be recorded permanently then magnetic tape recorders or hard disk drives can be used. [8]

There are different types of dynamic inputs, which are described below.

1. Periodic input:

The periodic input varies cyclically with time or repeating itself after a constant interval of time. The input may be harmonic or non harmonic.

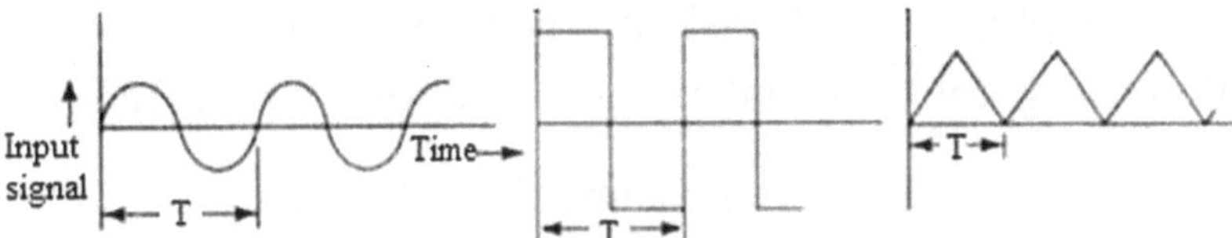

Figure: Periodic signal with time period T

2. Transient input:

The transient input varies non cyclically with time. It is the short duration signal. The signal is of a definite duration and become zero after a certain period.

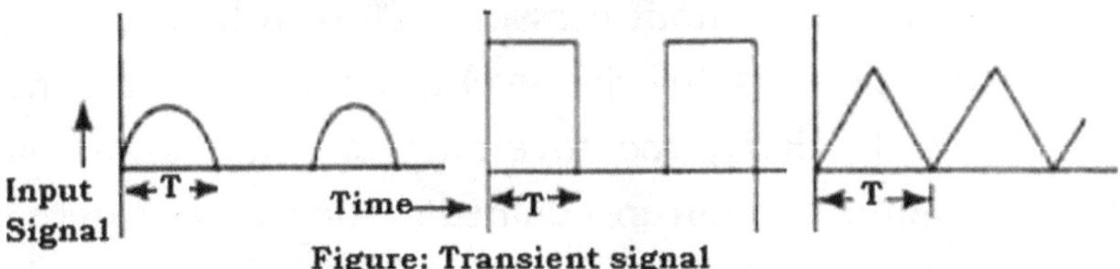

Figure: Transient signal

3. Random input:

The random input varies randomly with time. This input has no definite period and no definite amplitude. This input may be continuous but not cyclic.

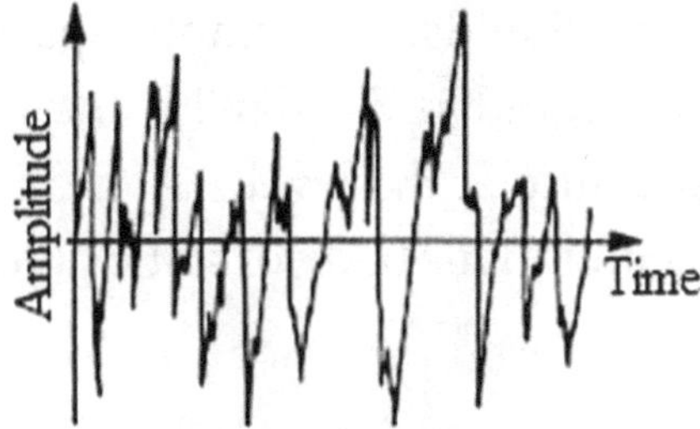

Figure: Random signal

The vibration excitation due to unbalance of a rotating body is periodic or harmonic, the pressure variations is an internal combustion engine is periodic while forces due to an explosion are transient. The pressure fluctuations in fluid flow due to turbulence are of random type. [10]

To study dynamic characteristics of instrument, it is necessary to represents each instrument by its mathematical model. The governing equations or relation between output and input can be obtained and is called as the formulation of equation of system.

1.5: The governing equation of U-tube manometer:

In manometer, the input pressure "P" is to be measured while the output is "h" the level difference between the two tubes. To derive the governing equation, the initial forces of liquid column are equated to some of the external forces due to pressure, gravity and friction between tube walls and fluid.

Therefore, inertial force = Pressure force + friction force+ gravity force.

The U- tube manometer is used for measuring pressure differences in the liquids. The empty space in both the limbs above the liquid is filled with the air. Therefore, equating the pressure at the level AA′ i.e. Pressure at the same level in a continuous body of static fluid is equal. [11]

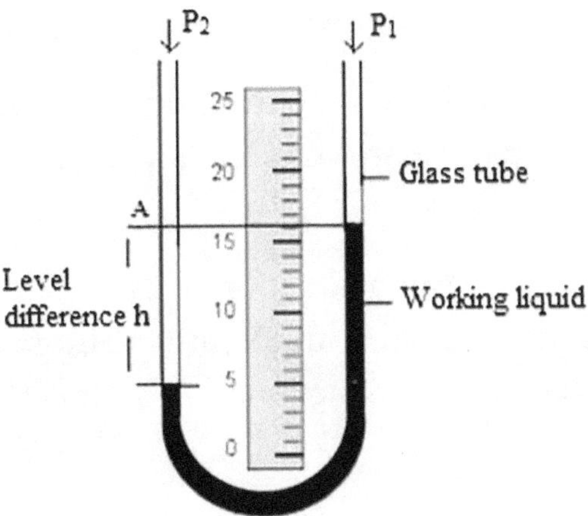

Figure: U-tube manometer

As shown in above figure,

For the right hand side of the manometer,

$P = P_1 - \rho g\,(h+a)$,

Similarly, for left hand side it is,

$P' = P_2 - (\rho xgh + \rho ga)$,

Since $P' = P$,

We get,

$P_1 - \rho g\,(h+a) = P_2 - (\rho xgh + \rho ga)$,

$P_1 - P_2 = \rho g\,(h+a) - (\rho xgh + \rho ga)$,

$P_1 - P_2 = \rho gh - \rho xgh$

$P_1 - P_2 = (\rho - \rho x)\,gh$,

If $\rho x <<< \rho$, then we can write,

$P_1 - P_2 = \rho gh$.

1.6: A display unit connected by resistance transducer:

A resistance transducer is connecting to display unit, the resistor and capacitor are connected in circuit as shown in following figure.

To derive the governing equation of the input and output voltages, let us assume, V_1 and V_2 are the input and output voltage respectively, are the function of time t. [7]

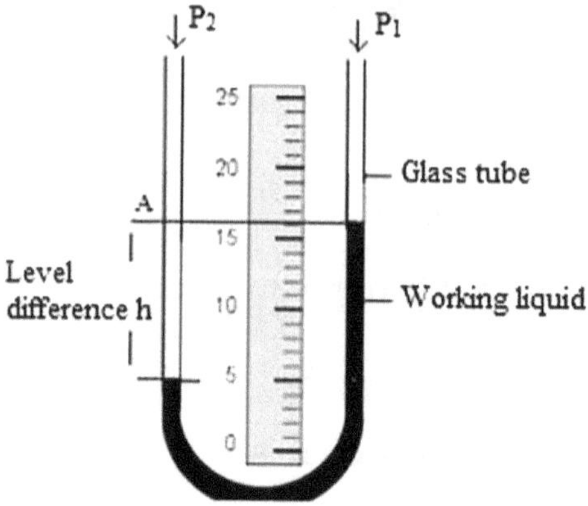

If Z be the impedance of the display which is given as,

$$\frac{1}{Z} = \frac{1}{R} + \frac{1}{1/DC} \quad \text{---------(1)}$$

$$\frac{1}{Z} = \frac{1}{R} + DC \quad \text{---------(2)}$$

Where, $D = d/dt$

We have, $$\frac{V_2}{V_1} = \frac{Z}{Ri + Z} \quad \text{---------(3)}$$

From equations 1 and 3, we can write,

$$\frac{V_2}{V_1} = \frac{1}{1 + Ri\left(\frac{1}{R} + DC\right)}$$

This can be written as,

$$V_2(1 + \tau D) = V_1 \text{------------ (4)} \qquad \text{Where, } \tau = Ri.C$$

It is to be supposed that, the value of Ri/R is very small so it can be neglected. Equation 4 is the first order equation, related to the input and output and can be written as,

$$\frac{dV_2}{dt} + V_2 = V_1$$

References

1. Static and dynamic characteristics of instruments, iitdelhi, PMV Subbarao.

2. fetweb.ju.edu.jo/staff/me/jyamin/measurent course/ instrument.

3. HGSI the sensor connection, Harold G Schaevitz industries LLC.

4. http://hyperphysics.phy-astr.gsu.edu/hbase/solids/ hyst.

5. www.ndeed.org/EducationResources/ CommunityCollege/MagParticle/Physics/ HysteresisLoop

6. www.mechanicalhero.com/2012/10/classification of instruments by mechguru.

7. Instrumentation: measurement and analysis by B.C.Nakra and k.k.Chaudhary.

8. www.indiastudychannel.com/resources/139106-Functional-Elements-an-Instrument.

9. http://mvs-mm.blogspot.in/2013/02/dynamic-inputs.

10. www.linuxfocus.org/English/March2003/article271.

11. www.acmasindia.com/blog/manometer

2. Basic principles of Measurement

2.1: Introduction:

The researchers in different parts of the country or world may compare the results of their experiments on a regular basis. It is necessary to establish certain standard units of length, weight, time, temperature and electrical, quantities. The National Bureau of Standards has the primary responsibility for maintaining these standards, The Indian Standard Institute (ISI); New Delhi has taken the responsibility for maintaining the entire measurements standard in India. To supervise the standard of measurements, the same Institute deliver instructions to put ISI mark on the measuring instruments and items so that these may be compared with non-standard ones. The ISO (International Standards Organization) is also one of the organization works to maintain the standards. ISO International Standards Organization ensure that products and services are safe, reliable and of good quality.

2.2: Units:

A unit of measurement is a definite quantity, defined and adopted by convention and used as a standard for measurement of the same physical quantity. In the measurement system, the quantity to be measured is compared directly against a standard of same kind of quantity. The magnitude of quantity being measured is expressed in terms of a chosen unit for the standard and a numerical multiplier. A weight can be measured in terms of Kilograms and a numerical constant. Thus, a 5 Kilogram weight means a weight five times greater than a kilogram.

There are two classes of units in the SI system, the basic units and derived units. The basic units provide the reference used to define all the measurement units of the system and the derived units are the products of base units and are used as a measure of derived quantities. There are seven basic (fundamental) units, which are given below. [1,2,3,]

Derived quantity	Unit	
Area	Square meter	m^2
Volume	Cubic meter	m^3
Speed, velocity	Meter per second	m/s
Acceleration	Meter per second square	m/s^2
Density, mass density	Kilogram per cubic meter	kg/m^3
Magnetic field strength	Ampere per meter	A/m
Specific volume	Cubic meter per kilogram	m^3/kg

2.2.1: The basic (standard) units:

Length:

The meter is considered as one of the fundamental unit, its SI unit is meter. The standard meter is defined as the length of a platinum-iridium bar maintained at very accurate conditions at the International Bureau of Weights and Measures at France. All other meters had to be calibrated against the meter. The conversion factor for length is, 1 meter = 39.37 inches. At the National Bureau of Standards, Secondary standard of length is maintained for calibration purposes. In 1960, the general conference on weights and measures defined the standard meter in terms of the wavelength of the orange-red light of a krypton-86 lamp. The standard meter is 1 meter = 1,650,763.73 wavelengths of orange-red light of Krypton-86. After some years, i.e. in 1982, the definition of the meter was defined as the distance light travels in 1/299,792,458ths of a second. Centimeter is the fundamental unit of length in CGS system. Its conversion factors for other system are already mentioned above. The derived units for length are as follows:

$1 \text{ m} = 10^2 \text{ cm}$,

$1 \text{ centimeter} = 10^{-2} \text{ m}$

$1 \text{ km} = 10^5 \text{ cm} = 1000 \text{ m}$

$1 \text{ mm} = 10^{-3} \text{ m} = 10^{-1} \text{ cm}$

$1 \text{ decimeter} = 10^{-1} \text{ m}$

$1 \text{ decameter} = 10 \text{ m}$

$1 \text{ hectometer} = 10^2 \text{ m}$.

Weight:

The SI unit of mass is kilogram. The standard kilogram is defined in terms of platinum-iridium mass maintained at very accurate conditions at the International Bureau of Weights and Measures in France.

1 pound = 453.59237 grams = 0.45359237 kilogram

The National Bureau of Standards maintained the Secondary standard of mass for calibration purpose. In MKS and SI systems, fundamental unit of mass is kilogram, whereas in CGS system, the unit for the mass is gram.

1 kilogram = 10^3 grams; 1 gram = 10^{-3} kilogram
1 hectogram = 100 grams = 10^{-1} kilogram
1 decagram = 10 grams = 10^{-2} kilogram
1 milligram = 0.001 gram = 10^{-6} kilogram

Time:

The SI unit of time is second and has been defined in the past as of a mean solar day. The solar day is measured as the time interval between successive travels of the sun across a meridian of the earth. The time interval varies with location of the earth and time of the year, however, the mean solar day for one year is constant.

The standard units of time are established in terms of known frequencies of oscillation of pendulum. An electric clock uses 50Hz frequency as a standard because it operates from a synchronous electric motor whose speed depends on line frequency.

Temperature:

In 1854 Lord Kelvin was proposed an absolute temperature scale and forms the basis for thermodynamic calculations. The International Practical Temperature scales are furnishes on an experimental basis for a temperature scale which approximates as closely as possible the absolute thermodynamic temperature scale. In the International Scale, according to freezing (0°C) and boiling point of the water (100°C) the temperature scales are established.

Luminous intensity:

Candela is the SI unit of luminous intensity of a source of light in a specified direction. The candela is the luminous intensity of a black body of surface area $1/60,000$ m^2 placed at the temperature of freezing platinum and at a pressure of $101,325$ N/m^2, in the direction perpendicular to its surface. Now candela is redefined as the luminous intensity in a given direction of a source that emits monochromatic radiation of frequency 540 ´ 1012 Hz and that has a radiant intensity in that direction of $1/683$ watt per steradian. (SI unit of solid angle). [4, 5]

2.2.2: Derived Units:

The units of all other physical quantities can be expressed in terms of these base units in combination. For example, the unit of speed is meter per second, the unit of density in kilogram per cubic meter. Let us consider another physical quantity like force. The force can be defined as the product of mass and acceleration, therefore the unit of force is taken as $Kg.m/S^2$, called as "Newton" on behalf of his work. The unit of energy is Newton-meter say, Joule. The unit of power is Joule per second, called as a Watt.

2.3: Standards of measurement:

The measurement is the physical representation of the quantity. The physical representation of the units of the measurement is the standard of measurement. Following two requirements should ask during the measurement.

1) The measurement which is used for comparison must be will established, highly accurate and reproducible.
2) The measurement devices and calibration processes used must have a true reliability.

There are different types of standards of measurement. They can be classified according to their function and type of application.

1. Standard:

A standard is a known accurate measure of physical quantity. Standards are used to determine the values of other physical quantities by the comparison method. All standards are preserved at the International Bureau of Weight and Measures, which is situated in France, Paris.

There are four categories of standards,

1. International Standard.
2. Primary Standard.

3. Secondary Standard.

4. Working Standard

International Standard is defined by International agreement which represent the closest possible accuracy attainable by the current science and technology

Primary Standard is maintained at the National Standard Laboratory (different for every country). The function of primary standard is the calibration and verification of secondary Standard. Secondary Standard is the Basic reference Standard used by measurement and calibration in the laboratories and in industries and is maintained by the particular industry. Each laboratory has its own secondary Standard which are periodically checked and certified by the National Standard Laboratory. Working Standard is the Principal tools of a measurement in the laboratory. It is Used to check and calibrate laboratory instrument for accuracy and performance. For example, Standard resistor for checking the resistance value manufactured.

1. International standard:

The international standards are designed and constructed to the specification of an international forum. It represents the units of measurement of various physical quantities to the highest possible accuracy i.e. attainable by the use of advance technique of production and measurement technology. These standards are maintained by international bureau of weight and measures at France. For example, the international prototype kilogram is taken as the standard for weight; the wavelength of k_r^{36} orange red lamp for length and the cesium clock are the international standards for time. However these standards are not easily available to an ordinary user for purposes of day to day comparison and calibration.

2. Primary standard:

The primary standards or National standards are maintained by standard organizations like the National laboratory in different part of the world. These devices are representing the fundamental and derived quantities. These standards are calibrated independently by absolute measurement. The main function of these standards is to calibrate and/or check and certify the secondary standards. These standards are also not easily available to an ordinary uses for verification and/or calibration of working standard.

3. Secondary standard:

These standards are basic reference standard, used in industries. These standards are maintained by the particular involved industry and are checked locally against other reference standards in that particular area. The responsibility of these standards is to maintain and calibrate the secondary standards entirely with the industrial laboratory itself. These standards should periodically send to the National standard laboratories for calibration and comparison against the primary standards.

4. Working standard:

The working standards are highly accurate devices which are commercially available. These standards are dually check and certified against other the primary or secondary standards. For example, the most widely used industrial working standard of length is the precision gauge blocks, which are made up of steel. Similarly a standard are cell and a standard resistor are the working standard of voltage and resistance respectively. These standard are widely used for calibrating general laboratory instrument for carrying out comparison measurement or for checking the quality (range of which is already decided) of industrial product. [6]

2.4: Calibration:

A known input is given to the measurement system and the systems output is noted. if the systems output deviates with respect to the given known input, corrections are made in the instrument so that the output matches the input. This process is called calibration.

To calibrate means to determine, check, or rectify the graduation of any instrument giving quantitative measurements. To calibrate means to divide or mark with gradations, graduations, or other indexes of degree, quantity. To calibrate means to plan or devise (something) carefully so as to have a precise use, application, appeal, etc.

The calibration is the result of quantitative comparison between standard and the output of measuring system measuring the same quantity. If the output -input response of the system is linear then a single point calibration is sufficient, wherein only a single known standard value of the input is employed. However if the system response is non-linear set of known standard input to the measuring system are employed for calibrating the corresponding output of the system. Different type of calibration is classified as follows.

1. Primary calibration:

A system is calibrated against the primary standard are called primary calibration. The standard resistors or standard cells are available for the measurement of standard resistance and voltage measurement respectively.

2. Secondary calibration:

The process is called secondary calibration when it is used for further secondary calibrating another device of lesser accuracy. These are widely used in general laboratories, factories as well as in industries.

3. Direct calibration with known input source:

The accuracy of this is as that of primary calibration. Therefore device that are calibrated directly are also used as secondary calibrating devices for example, flow meter such as turbine flow meter may directly calibrated by using primary measurements.

2.5: Error:

The error is the deviation from the true value of the measured variable. Precision is composed of two characteristics, conformity and the number of significant figures to which measurement may be made. For example, the value of resistor 1448676Ω, when is measured by an ohmmeter it consistently and repeatedly indicates 1.5 MΩ, this is close to the true value. This type of error is created because of the limitations of the scale and is also called as a precision error. Significant figures convey actual information regarding the magnitude and precision of quantity. More significant figure represents greater precision of Measurement. It means that, the conformity is necessary but not sufficient.

Types of static error:

1) Gross error (human error)
2) Systematic Error
3) Random Error

1. Gross Error:

These errors are caused by human mistakes in reading or using instruments. These errors cannot eliminate but can minimize.

2. Systematic Error:

These errors are due to shortcomings of the instrument, such as defective or damaged parts.

The systematic errors are subdivided into three types,

a. Instrumental error
b. Environmental error.
c. Observational error

a. Instrumental error:

This type of error introduced because of the mechanical structure (bearing friction, irregular spring tension, stretching of spring, etc). The errors can be avoided by selecting a suitable instrument for the particular measurement, applying correction factor, by determining instrumental error and calibrating the instrument against the desired standard.

b. Environmental error:

This type of error introduced due to external atmospheric conditions such as change in temperature, humidity, barometer pressure, etc including surrounding area condition affects the measurement. The error can be avoided

By using the air conditioner, sealing certain component in the instruments and using the magnetic shields.

c. Observational error:

This type of error is commonly introduced by the observer, for example, misreading of the scale, parallax error and estimation error.

3. Random error:

This type of error introduces due to unknown causes and so called as a random error. This type of error occurs when all systematic error has accounted accumulation of small effect, require at high degree of accuracy.

This type of error can be avoided by increasing number of reading and using statistical means to obtain best approximation of true value. [7]

References

1. www.french-metrology.com/en/si/units-measurement.asp

2. www.edinformatics.com/math_science/units.htm.

3. http://physics.about.com/od/toolsofthetrade/a/SIunits.

4. http://www.ignou.ac.in/upload/Unit-1-62.pdf

5. G.K.Vijauraghavan, Engineering metrology and measurement by, ARS publication.

6. B.C.Nakra and k.k.Chaudhary, Instrumentation: measurement and analysis.

7. www.ignou.ac.in/upload/unit-2-62 pdf.

3. Transducers

3.1: Introduction

Instrumentation is the heart of industrial applications. Instrumentation is the art and science of measuring and controlling different variables such as flow, level, temperature, angle, displacement etc. A basic instrumentation system consists of various devices. One of these various devices is a transducer. A transducer plays a very important role in any instrumentation system.

A transducer is an electronic device that converts energy from one form to another. The well known examples are microphones, loudspeakers, thermometers, pressure sensors, antenna etc. A transducer is a device which is capable of converting the physical quantity into a proportional electrical quantity such as voltage or electric current. Hence it converts any quantity to be measured into usable electrical signal. This physical quantity which is to be measured can be pressure, level, temperature, displacement etc. The output which is obtained from the transducer is in the electrical form and is equivalent to the measured quantity. For example, a temperature transducer will convert temperature to an equivalent electrical potential. This output signal can be used to control the physical quantity or display it.

As efficiency of transducer is an important parameter it can be defined as the ratio of the power output in the desired form to the total power input and is always represents in percentage. Mathematically, $E = Q/P$

If P is the total input power and Q is the power output in the desired form

Till to date there is no transducer which can give 100 percent efficiency. Some power is always lost in the conversion the process. Usually this loss is obviously in the form of heat. A 100-watt bulb radiates only a few watts in the form of visible light. Most of the power is dissipated as heat; a small amount is radiated in ultraviolet spectrum. [1, 2, 3]

3.2: Types of transducers:

Electromagnetic transducer: The Magnetic cartridge converts relative physical motion into electrical signals, the Hall Effect sensor converts a magnetic field level into an electrical signal, magnetic tape recorder converts magnetic fields on a magnetic medium into electrical signals.

Electrochemical transducer: pH probes, Electro-galvanic fuel cell etc.

Electromechanical transducer: Relative motion through magnetic field will produce voltage at the end of the conductor. Strain gauge, Accelerometer Galvanometer, Rotary motor, linear motor, Linear variable differential transformer etc.

Photoelectric transducer: Light-emitting diode – converts electrical power into incoherent light, Laser Diode – converts electrical power into coherent light, Photodiode – converts changing light levels into electrical signals, Photo detector or light dependent resistor (LDR) – converts changes in light levels into changes in electrical resistance, Fluorescent and Incandescent lamp – converts electrical power into incoherent light.

Thermoelectric transducer: Resistance temperature detector (RTD) – converts temperature into an electrical resistance signal. Thermocouple – converts relative temperatures of metallic junctions to electrical voltage, thermistor etc.

Electro acoustic transducer: Microphone – converts sound into an electrical signal, Loudspeaker, earphone – converts electrical signals into sound, Piezoelectric crystal – converts deformations of solid-state crystals i.e. vibrations to and from electrical signals. The Ultrasonic transreceiver transmitting the ultrasound as well as receiving it after sound reflection from target objects, availing for imaging of those objects.

Transducers are broadly classified in to two types, Active transducer and Passive transducer.

Active Transducer:

Active transducers are those which do not require any power source for their operation. They work on the energy conversion principle. They produce an electrical signal proportional to the input. For example, a thermocouple, a device used to measure temperature is an active transducer.

Passive Transducers:

Transducers which require an external power source for their operation is called as a passive transducer. They produce an output signal in the form of some variations in the resistance, capacitance or any other parameter which can be converted into equivalent current or voltage signal. For example, a photocell is a passive transducer which varies the resistance of the cell when light incident on it. This change in resistance is converted to proportional signal with the help of a bridge circuit. Hence a photocell can be used to measure the intensity of light.

The bonded strain gauge is a passive transducer which is used to measure stress or pressure. As the stress on the strain gauge increases or decreases the strain gauge bends or compresses causing the resistance of the wire bonded on it to increase or decrease. The change in resistance which is equivalent to the change in stress is measured with the help of a bridge. Hence stress is measured.

While selecting transducers the following characteristic should take into account. Selection criteria of a transducer are based on different factors, such as availability, cost, power consumption, environmental conditions, etc. After considering these entire factors one can select a best one for our use.

Selection of the transducer among the many available mainly depends upon the Input characteristics, Transfer characteristics and Output characteristics.

3.3: Characteristics of Transducer:

The following factors should take into account, while selecting a transducer for any application.

Input characteristics:

While selecting a transducer, this is one of the most important characteristic. These characteristics determine which type of input is needed for that particular transducer. What is the operating range for that transducer and what will be the loading effect on that transducer.

Transfer characteristics:

Transfer characteristics means, the effects on the signal when it is being processed. Transfer characteristics also plays very important role in selection of transducer. When the signal is being processed the errors and hysteresis can occurs. Some transfer characteristics should take into account while selecting a transducer for any purpose i.e. Accuracy and precision Calibration Error and hysteresis Response of transducer to the environment influences.

Output characteristics:

The output characteristics play a very important role while selecting a special type of transducer. Some of the output characteristics are type of output, purpose, output impedance, useful range, availability, cost, life span, stability and reliability.

3.4: Strain gage:

The purpose of strain gauges is to measure extremely small displacements, of the order of nanometers. When a fine wire, within its elastic limit, (25 µm) is strained, the resistance of wire changes because of changes in the diameter, length and resistivity. The Wheatstone bridge circuit is ideal for measuring small changes in resistance.

The most popular electrical elements used in force measurements include the resistance strain gage, the semiconductor strain gage, and piezoelectric transducers. The strain gage measures force indirectly by measuring the deflection it produces in a calibrated carrier. Pressure can be converted into a force using an appropriate transducer, and strain gage techniques can then be used to measure pressure. Flow rates can be measured using differential pressure measurements which also make use of strain gage technology.

The resistance strain gage is a resistive element which changes in length, hence resistance, as the force applied to the base on which it is mounted causes stretching or compression. It is perhaps the most well known transducer for converting force into an electrical variable.

Strain Gauge is an example of passive transducer that uses the variation in electrical resistances in wires to sense the strain produced by a force on the wires.[4]

Since Strain can be measure more easily by using variable resistance transducers, it is common practice to measure strain instead of stress. If a metal conductor is stretched or compressed its resistance changes on account of the fact that both the length and diameter of conductor changes. Also there is a change in value of resistivity of the conductor when subjected to strain, a property called as resistive effect. Therefore resistance Strain Gauge is also known as piezo resistive gauges. Many transducers load cells, torque meters, pressure gauges, temperature sensors etc. employ strain gauges as secondary transducer. Two types of strain gauges are discussed below.

3.4.1: Unbounded resistance wire strain gauge:

The unbounded strain gages consist of a wire stretched between two parts in an insulating medium such as air. The diameter of wire is about 25 µm; the wires are kept under tension so that there is no sag and pre vibration. (as in following figure) Unbounded strain gauges are usually connected in bridge circuit. The bridge is balance with no load applied.

When external load is applied to the strain gage the resistance of strain gauge changes. This resistance change unbalances the bridge circuit, which changes the output voltage. This voltage is proportional to the strain. A Displacement of the order of 50 µm can be detected with these strain gauges.

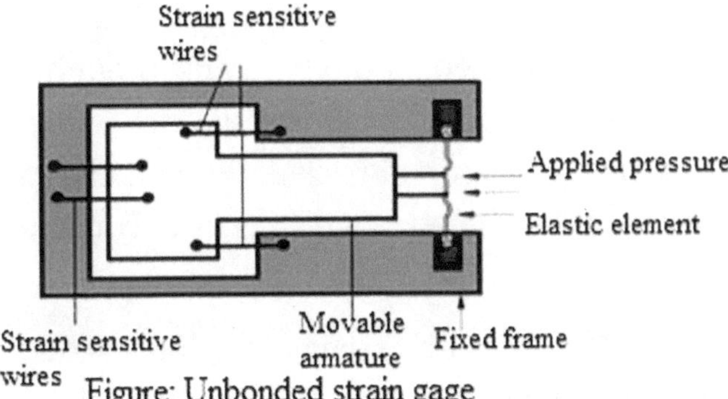

Figure: Unbonded strain gage

Force acting on the wire which having the area = A, length = L and resistivity = ρ will cause the wire to elongate or shorten, So that the resistance increase or decrease proportionally according to:

$R = \rho L / A$

And $\Delta R / R = GF \cdot \Delta L / L,$

Where GF = Gage factor (2.0 to 4.5 for metals, and greater than 150 for semiconductors. The dimensionless quantity $\Delta L/L$ is a measure of the force applied to the wire and is expressed in microstrains which are the same as parts-per-million (ppm). From the above equation, it is clear that larger the gage factor, larger resistance changes, hence, more sensitivity.

3.4.2: Bonded resistance wire strain gauge:

Bonded strain gages consist of a thin wire or conducting film arranged in a coplanar pattern and cemented to a base or carrier. The gage is normally mounted so that as much as possible of the length of the conductor is aligned in the direction of the stress that is being measured. Lead wires are attached to the base and brought out for interconnection. It consist of a fine resistance wire of about 25um in diameter is looped back and forth on a carrier is (base) or mounting the plate which is usually cemented to the main bar undergoing stress.

The greed of fine wire is cemented on carrier which may be a thin sheet of paper, Bakelite or Teflon wire is covered on the top with a thin material so that it is not damaged mechanically. The spreading of wires permits uniform distribution of stress. The carrier is then bonded or cemented to the member being studied this permits (to allow) good transfer of stress for carrier to wire.[5,6,7,8]

A tensile stress tends to elongate the wire and thereby increase length and decrease its cross sectional area, the combined effect is an increase in resistance as seen from following equation.

$$R = \rho L / A$$

Where, ρ- Specific resistance of material in ohm meter,

L - Length of conductor in meter, A- Area of cross sectional conductor in m^2

Bonded devices are considerably more practical and are in much wider use than unbounded devices. The most popular version of the bonded strain gage is the foil-type gage, produced by photo-etching techniques, and using similar metals to the wire types alloys of copper-nickel (Constantan), nickel-chromium (Nichrome), nickel-iron, platinum-tungsten, etc.

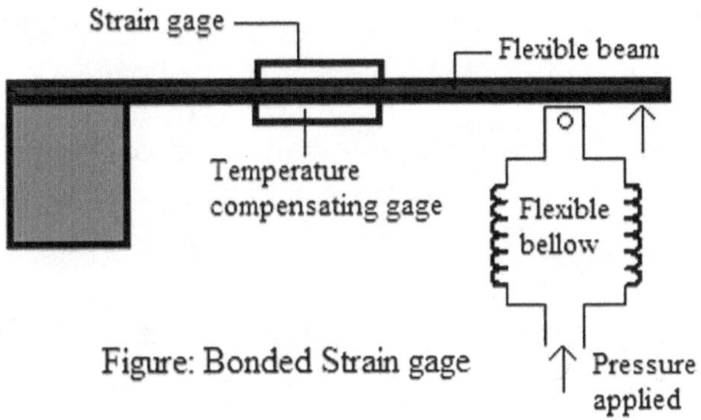

Figure: Bonded Strain gage

Gages having wire sensing elements present a small surface area to the specimen; this reduces leakage currents at high temperatures and permits higher isolation potentials between the sensing element and the specimen. Foil sensing elements, on the other hand, have a large ratio of surface area to cross-sectional area and are more stable under extremes of temperature and prolonged loading. The large surface area and thin cross section also permit the device to follow the specimen temperature and facilitate the dissipation of self-induced heat.

The resistance wire strain gauge should have following characteristic:-

1. It should have a high value of gauge factor; a high value of k indicates large change in resistance, strain resulting in high sensitivity

2. The strain gauge resistance should be as high as possible since this minimizes the effect of undesirable variations of resistance in the measurement circuit.

3. Strain gauge should not have any hysteresis effect in its response.

4. In order to maintain constancy of calibration over the entire range of strain gauge it should have linear characteristics

5. Strain gauges are frequently used for dynamic measurement and hence frequency response should be good. [9]

3.4.3: Semiconductor strain gages:

Semiconductor strain gages make use of the piezoresistive effect. In some semiconductor materials, for example, silicon and germanium this piezoresistive effect is used in order to obtain greater sensitivity and higher-level output. When strain is applied semiconductor gages can be produced to either positive or negative changes. Their change in resistance with strain is also nonlinear. They can be made physically small while still maintaining a high nominal resistance. Semiconductor strain gage bridges may have 30 times the sensitivity of bridges employing metal films, but are temperature sensitive and difficult to compensate. They are not in as widespread use as the more stable metal film devices for precision work; however, where sensitivity is important and temperature variations for metal-film bridges but is less critical because of the higher signal levels and decreased transducer accuracy. [10]

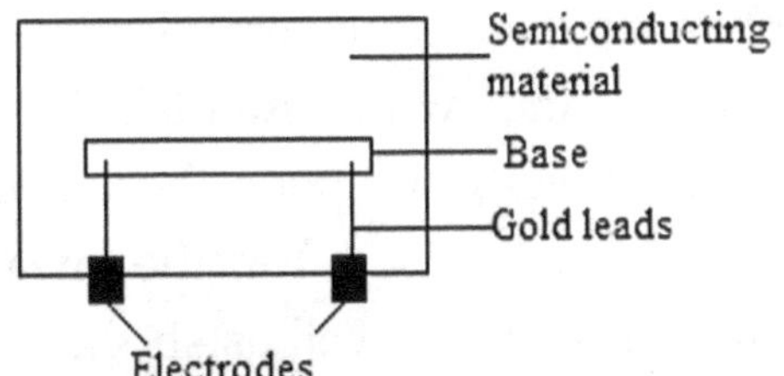

Figure: Semiconductor Strain gage

3.4.4: Piezoelectric force transducers:

A stress distribution in the crystal will be depends not only on the load applied but also the manner in which it applied and upon the size and shape of the sensing element. Such devices find wide application in the measurement of pressure and force. The important parameter considered is sensitivity, natural frequency, non-frequency hysteresis, temperature effect, acceleration, response and cross sensitivity. The performance of crystal element depend upon the magnitude of crystals piezoelectric constants.

The most popular piezoelectric material having significant value of piezoelectric constant and sensitivity are natural quartz's, Rochelle salt, variety of synthetic ceramic material like Barium titanate and lead zirconate titanate, are piezo electric materials. The natural quartz's is the most stable device for many applications. It has lower temperature sensitivity and a higher sensitivity, this giving an inherently long time constant which permits static calibration. Further it exhibits good linearity over a wide range of stress level with very low hysteresis.

On the other hand, piezoelectric ceramic have considerably higher sensitivity and wide adaptability though the temperature characteristic are poor. Piezoelectric pressure transducers are widely used for the measurement of rapidly varying pressure as well as shock pressure. They provide flat frequency response from 1 Hz to 20 KHz. The various configurations under which the piezoelectric transducer material can be applied for pressure and force measurement are given in following figure.

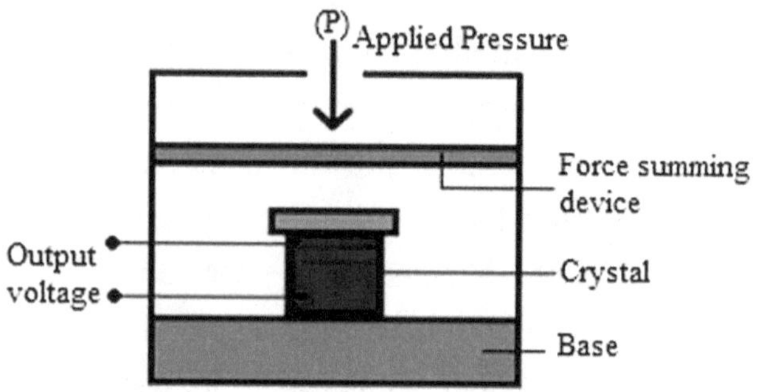

Figure: Piezo-electric transducer

Certain types of materials generate an electrostatic charge or voltage. A piezoelectric transducer is a device that transforms one type of energy to another. When a piezoelectric material is subjected to stress or force, it generates an electrical signal; it may be potential or voltage and is proportional to the magnitude of the force. This type of transducer can be a converter of mechanical energy or force into electric potential. When pressure is applied to the crystal, it results into the mechanical deformation. This property of piezoelectric has been utilized in the design of pressure transducer; where in the mechanical stress is generated by diaphragm subjected to pressure. A stress distribution in the crystal will be depends not only on the load applied but also the manner in which it applied and upon the size and shape of the sensing element. Such devices find wide application in the measurement of pressure and force. The important parameter considered is sensitivity, natural frequency, non-frequency hysteresis, temperature effect, acceleration, response and cross sensitivity. The performance of crystal element depend upon the magnitude of crystals piezoelectric constants.

In microphones these transducers are useful because of the high sensitivity, where they convert sound pressure into electric voltage. In precision balances, in accelerometers, motion detectors and ultrasound generators / detectors these are used. They are also used in non-destructive testing, in the generation of high voltages.

When a voltage is applied to a piezoelectric material it get bent, stretched, or otherwise deformed. This deformation is usually very minor and proportional to the voltage applied. Hence, this type of transducer can also be used as an actuator for the exact adjustment of fine optical instruments, lasers, and atomic force microscopes.

These devices can be used both as sensors and actuators, so they're referred to as transducers. We know, transducer is a device that can convert one form of energy into another.

As a result, both piezoelectric sensors and actuators are transducer. The sensor turns mechanical energy into electric potential and the actuator converts electrical energy into mechanical force or motion.

The voltage generated by piezoelectric transducers can be quite high, approximately thousands of volts, when the material is initially deformed. This property has been used in electronic cigarette lighters and push-button igniters for gas ranges and grills. In these applications, pushing a button activates a small, spring-loaded hammer, which strikes a piezoelectric material and generates a voltage sufficient to cause an electric arc to jump between the exposed electrodes of the igniter.

The specific types of crystals like quartz and topaz are the piezoelectric materials. Now a day, polymers and ceramics also shows the piezoelectric properties. The most common piezoelectric material currently in use is the man-made ceramic lead zirconate titanate (PZT). This material has the ability to provide twice the voltage of quartz under a given force.

These transducers are very simple, reliable and very strong, and so are widely use in industry, medicine, and aero-space work. These transducers are not affected by external electromagnetic fields, and so can be used in applications where electronic sensors would not succeed. They are very stable over a broad range of temperatures and can be affected by high temperatures, when used for long time.

3.4.5: Linear Variable Differential Transducer (LVDT):

It is a passive inductive transducer the basic construction of which is shown as the following figure. It consist single primary windings and two secondary windings S_1 and S2 wound on a hollow cylindrical former. The secondary's having equaled number of turns and identical placed on either side of primary. Primary is connected to source. A movable iron core slides with the hollow former and therefore affects the magnetic coupling between primary and both the secondary's.

The displacement to be measured is applied to an arm attached to the iron core. To reduce the eddy current loss, the core is made up of Ni-Fe alloy. Equal voltages are induced in both the secondary's, when the core is in its normal position or null position. The frequency of the Ac mains applied to the primary winding is 50 KHz. Both the windings are connected in series opposition to convert the output from both secondary windings into a single signal as shown in following figure.

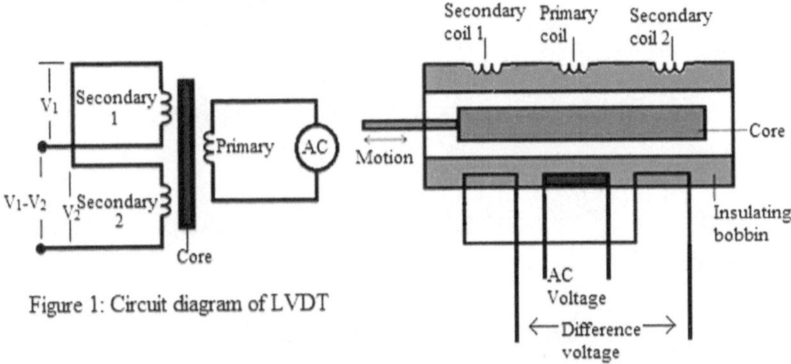

Figure 1: Circuit diagram of LVDT

Figure: Schematic diagram of LVDT

Hence the output voltage of the transducer is the difference of two voltages. Therefore the differential output voltage i. e. E_o

At its normal position of core a flux linking both secondary's is equal. Therefore the EMF induced in them is also equal i.e. at null position $Es_1 = Es_2$ i.e. output voltage of transformer E_o = Zero (O)

If core is move to S_1 from null position, Then, flux $Es_1 > Es_2$ therefore the magnitude of output voltage is $Es_1 = Es_2$ in phase with Es_2.

The amount of voltage change in either secondary winding is proportional to the amount of movement of the core, gives the indication of amount of linear motion by counting which output is increasing or decreasing, the direction of motion can be determined. Hence the output voltage of LVDT is a linear function of core displacement within the limited range of motion (ray 5mm from the null position)

Advantages:

1. This transducer absorbs high degree of vibration and shocks.

2. The output is linear for very small displacement, up to 5mm.

3. The resolution is infinite; the change in output voltage is stepless.

4. The hysteresis loss is very less so the repeatability is excellent.

5. It does not require an amplifier, as its output is already high.

6. The sensitivity is very high, approximately 40 V/mm.

7. There are no sliding contacts, so no friction in the device.

8. The power consumption required is very low, less than 1W.

Limitations:

1) For appreciable output, large displacement is required.

2) These are sensitive to random magnetic fields.

3) The temperature variation affects the transducer.

4) The recovering instrument must be selected to operate on ac signals. [11, 12]

3.4.6: Potentiometric devices:

The variable resistance transducers are one of the most commonly used types of transducers. These transducers are also called as resistive transducers or sensors. They can be used for measuring various physical quantities like temperature, pressure, displacement, force, vibrations etc. These transducers are usually used as the secondary transducers, where the output from the primary mechanical transducer acts as the input for the variable resistance transducer. The output obtained from this transducer is calibrated against the input quantity which directly gives the value of the input.

The working principle of this type of transducer is that the resistance of the conductor is directly proportional to the length of the conductor and inversely proportional to the area of the conductor. Hence, if L is the length of the conductor and its area is A, then its resistance (in ohms) is given by: $R = \rho L/A$, Where ρ is called as resistivity of the material and it is constant for the materials and is measured in ohm-m. The resistance of some materials also changes with the change in their temperature. This principle is primarily used for the measurement of temperature.

Some Examples of the Variable Resistance Transducers are discussed below.

Wire resistance strain gauge: This device is used for the measurement of force, stress and strain. When the tension is applied to the electrical conductor, its length increases while the area of cross section decreases, due to which the resistance of the conductor changes. This change in resistance can be easily measured and can be calibrated against input. Sliding contact devices: In device, the length of the conductor is variable. One end of the conductor is fixed, while the position of the other end is decided by the slider or the brush which moves along the whole length of the conductor.

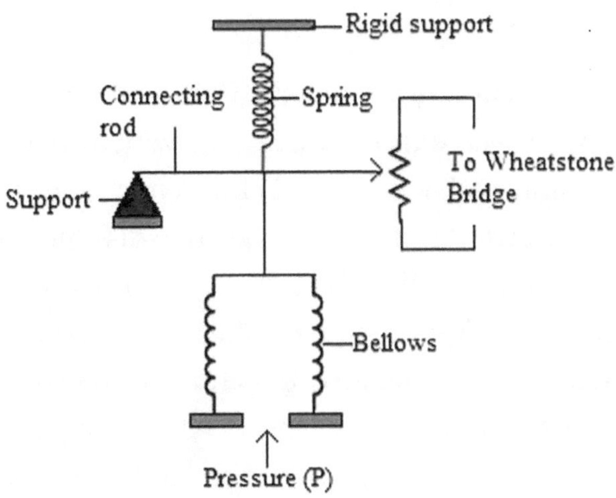

Figure: Potentiometric type transducer

The slider is connected to the body whose displacement is to be measured, obviously, when the body moves, the slider also moves along the conductor ultimately the length changes, so its resistance changes. The following figure depicts this type of device. The effective resistance is measured as the resistance between the fixed position of the conductor and the position of the sliding contact. These devices can be used to measured linear as well as angular displacement.[13]

Wire resistance strain gauge: This device is used for the measurement of force, stress and strain. When the tension is applied to the electrical conductor, its length increases while the cross section area decreases, due to which the resistance of the conductor changes. This change in resistance can be measured and is calibrated against the input.

3.5: Thermocouple:

Thermocouple is a very popular devise used for measurement of temperature. There are three effects on which thermocouple works, are the Seeback effect, Peltier effect and Thomson effect. Seeback effect states that, when two dissimilar metallic wires are joined at their ends the electromotive force exists at their junction. According to Peltier effect, the amount of electromotive force generated depends on the temperature of the junction, while Thomson effect tells us that the amount of voltage generated depends on the temperature gradient along the conductors in the circuit. The output voltage of the thermocouple changes as its temperature changes and this output voltage are calibrated against the temperature of the body that can be measured easily.

3.6: Thermistors:

Thermistors means thermal resistor, it works on the principle of the resistance change of some materials with the change in their temperature. When the temperature of the material changes, its resistance changes and can be measured and calibrated against the input quantity. Basically, the thermistors are made up of the ceramic like semiconducting materials such as oxides of manganese, nickel and cobalt. Thermistors can be used for the measurement of temperature, as electric power sensing devices and for the controls for various processes.

The main advantage of this type of pressure transducer are high range, ruggedness and simple instrumentation while finite resolution, limited life, large size, poor frequency response, tendency to develop noise as slider wears off and suspendability to vibration are some disadvantages.

Typical characteristic are, Resolution of 0.2% linearity of ± 1%, repeatability of ± 25% and hysteresis of ± 0.5 % all with to full scale range.

3.7: Digital Transducer:

It is possible to identify the position of movable test piece in terms of a binary numbers by the digital code. The position is converted into train of pulses. This is achieved by a digital transducer which is also term as encoder.

3.7.1: Optical encoder:

A sector may be design as shown in the following figure with a pattern of opaque and translucent areas. A photo sensor and a light source are placed on two sides of the sectors. When displacement is applied to the sector, obviously there is change in the amount of light falling on the photo electric sensor. The pattern of the illuminated sensor then carries the information to the location of sector as shown in figure. The number of levels in the encoder determines the accuracy with which the device operates.

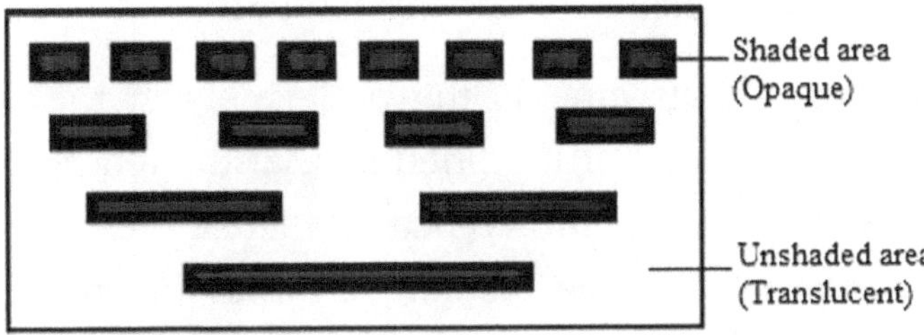

Figure : Rectangular Optical encoder

The advantages of this encoder are, they give a true digital read out. No mechanical contact involve and therefore no problem of wear and tear. The only drawback is the Light sources burns out. However the life of light is 5×10^4 hours.[14]

3.7.2: Resistive digital encoder:

In these method a pattern may be used the shaded areas made up of conducting material and unshaded areas of insulating material sliding contacts are used for making the contact circuit which come in contact with the conducting area are completed, while those which make contact with insulated areas are not completed. The encoder gives a digital read out, which is an indication of the position of the devices and hence determines the displacement.

The advantages of this type of encoders are, they are relatively inexpensive.

They can be made to any degree of accuracy desired, provided the sector is made large enough to accumulate the number of rows for binary numbers. The sectors are quite adequate for a slowly moving system. The drawbacks are, the Wear and tear contact causes error and there is often an ambiguity (not reliable of one digit in LSB).

For angular displacements the pattern given the above figure is to changed or modified so that the length of the scale becomes the circumference of a circle on a flat disc. The brushes are thin placed along a radial line in the disk as shown in following figure.

The disc is divided into concentric circular tracks each of which is then divided into segments in a manner depending upon the code being used. For pure binary code the inner most track is halved, the next quartered, the next divided into eight parts and so on. Each track has twice as many segments as the adjacent one near the centre. The detection method determines the treatment of the disc.

Alternate segment on each track are made transparent and opaque, if transmitted light and photocell are used. If the segments are reflecting and non- reflecting reflected light and photocell are used. Electrical methods are used for the detection in that case the segments are made alternating conducting and non-conducting (insulating).

3.7.3: Shaft encoder:

An optical encoder is an electromechanical device which has an electrical output in the digital form proportional to the angular position of the input shaft. The optical encoders make possible an angular displacement to be converted directly into a digital form. Therefore it is also called as an analog to digital converter. The digital encoder has four tracks (bit) and is divided into conducting and non-conducting position with smallest increment of 0.01mm. As the name suggest, optical encoders use light (optics) to identify unique positions for the encoder. There are four components in an optical shaft encoder:

1. A light source (LED).
2. A sensor.

3. A movable disc.

4. A fixed mask

The following figure clears the construction of optical encoder.

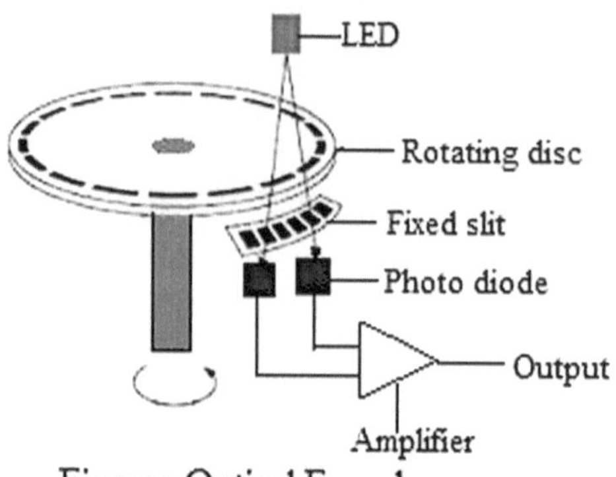

Figure : Optical Encoder

It has a shaft mechanically coupled to an input driver which rotates a disc rigidly fixed to it. A succession of opaque and translucent segments is marked on the surface of the disc. It works by shining light onto the edge of a disc outfitted with evenly spaced slits around the circumference. As the disc spins, light passes through the transparent slits and is blocked by the opaque spaces between the slits (the lamp circuits are made or broken). Light from infrared emitting diodes reaches the infrared receivers through the transparent slits of the rotating disc, an analogue signal is created. Then electronically, the signal is amplified and converted into digital form. This signal is then transmitted to the data processor.

The optical shaft encoder is used to measure both relative position and rotational distance traveled by a shaft. The encoder then detects how many slits have had light shine through, and in which direction the disk is spinning. To improve a robot in various ways the optical shaft encoder can be used. The encoder can measure rotational distance travelled and speed, which can be used to monitor, for example, the angular position of a robot gripper arm or the speed of a robot.

Applications:

The optical shaft encoder can be used to track distance traveled, direction of motion, or position of any rotary component. The encoder can also be used to detect movement, which could make easy interactions between the robot and its environment, for example human-robot interaction.[15, 16]

References

1. Whatis.techtarget.com › Topics › Computer Science › Electronics.

2. hyperphysics.phy-astr.gsu.edu/hbase/electronic/ transducer.

3. www.uvm.edu/~muse/modules/TDX/TDX1.pdf.

4. www.omega.com/prodinfo/straingages.html.

5. www.omega.com/literature/transactions/volume3/ images/strainfig05.gif.

6. www.instrumentationtoday.com/strain-gauge/2011/08/.Ref:

7. www.ibiblio.org/kuphaldt/electricCircuits/DC/DC_9.html.

8. Hareesh N.G, Introduction to strain gages, dayanand sagar College of enggineering, banglore.

9. www.globalspec.com/learnmore/sensors_transducers_detectors/pressure_sensing.

10. Semiconductor strain gage, http://www.ni.com/white-paper/14859/en/.

11. LVDT pressure sensors, http://www.sensorland.com/HowPage095, 2.

12. www.iamechatronics.com/notes/process-measurement/191-what-is-a-linear-variable-differential-transformer.

13. http://saba.kntu.ac.ir/eecd/ecourses/instrumentation/projects/reports/Pressure%20Sensor/Html/potentiometric_pressure_sensor.

14. Position sensor and linear positional sensors, www.electronics-tutorials.ws.

15. Techno box, Kawasaki heavy industrieshttps: //www.khi.co.jp /tb_e/07_ robot /07_robot).2.

16. www.ab.com/en/epub/catalogs/12772/6543185/12041221/12041235/Encoders

4. Data Acquisition System

4.1: Introduction:

All engineering activities require collection of data in development, production management, quality control, process control etc. To read the physical data scales, voltmeters, thermometer, oscilloscopes and such variety of measuring devices and instruments are used. Therefore there is an importance of data acquisition to systems/machines. Data acquisition is collecting data or information that describes the given situation. Modern data acquisition system interpret the real world signals into a format that digital computer can accept. It can regenerate the analog and other control signal from computer instruction. Most of real world data signal like temperature, pressure, flow, speed, intensity, position etc. cannot be read directly into electrical signal. For this purpose the transducers are used and the data is in the form of continuous analog output levels which are then to be interpreted into the digital form. The analog signal inputs to data acquisition systems are most often generated from sensors and transducers which convert the parameters such as pressure, temperature, stress or strain, flow, etc., into equivalent electrical signals. The electrically equivalent signals are then converted by the data acquisition system and are then utilized by the output devices in digital form. The ability of the electronic system to preserve signal accuracy and integrity is the main measure of the quality of the system. Data acquisition is generally relates to the process collecting the input data in digital form as rapidly, accurately and economically as necessary. Data acquisition and conversion systems are used to acquire analog signals from one or more sources and convert these signals into digital form for analysis or transmission by the devices such as digital computers, recorders, or communications networks. Data may be transmitted over long distance or short distance. A Data Acquisition system consists of sensors, data acquisition measurement hardware, and a computer with programmable software. Compared to traditional measurement systems, PC-based DAS systems develop the processing power, productivity, display and connectivity capabilities of industry standard computers providing a more powerful, flexible and cost-effective measurement solution. [1]

4.2. Basic Data Acquisition System:

A typical DAS consist of individual sensors with necessary signal conditioning, data conversion, data processing, multiplexing, data handling and associated transmission storage and display system. For converting analog information from more than one source either additional transducer or multiplexer are used to increase the speed with which information is accurately converted. The sample and hold circuit are also used. A schematic diagram of DAS is shown in following figure.

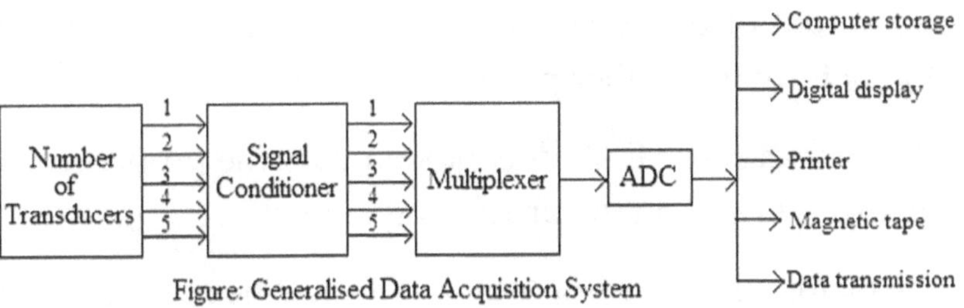

Figure: Generalised Data Acquisition System

The basic components required for the acquisition and conversion of analog signals into equivalent digital form are the following:

1. Transducers

2. Signal conditioners

3. Analog Multiplexer

4. Sample and hold circuit.

5. Analog-to-Digital Converter.

6. Output devices.

Typically, today's data acquisition systems contain all the elements needed for data acquisition and conversion, except, for input filtering and signal conditioning prior to analog multiplexing. The analog signals are time multiplexed by the analog multiplier; the multiplexer output signal is then usually applied to a very-linear fast-settling differential amplifier and/or to a fast-settling low aperture sample and hold circuit. The sample and hold circuit is programmed to acquire and hold each multiplexed data sample which is converted into digital form by an A to D converter. The converted sample is then presented at the output of the A to D converter in parallel and serial digital form for further processing by output devices.

The characteristic DAS depends on both the properties of analog data and on the processing carried out.

The factor which are important to decide the configuration and subsystem of DAS are as follows:

1. The accuracy and resolution.

2. The number of channel to monitored.

3. The rate of sampling per channel.

4. The signal conditioning requirement for each channel.

5. The Cost.

There are various configurations comprises as given below,

(A): The Single channel possibilities:

1. The Direct conversion.

2. The Pre amplification and direct conversion.

3. The Sample and hold conversion.

4. The Pre amplification signal conditioning and any of above.

(B): Multichannel Possibilities

1. Multiplexing the output of single channel converters.

2. Multiplexing the output of sample and hold circuits.

3. Multiplexing the input of sample and hold circuits.

4. Multiplexing the low level data.

Objective of DAS

1. At a correct speed and correct time it should acquire the necessary data.

2. It must be able to collect, summarized and stored data for dialysis of operation and record purpose.

3. To inform the operator about the state of plant all the data should use efficiently.

4. It must monitor to complete the plant to the operator to maintain on line optimum and safe operations.

5. It must provide an effective human communication system and be able to identify problem areas thereby minimizing unit availability maximizing unit through plant at minimum cost.

6. For future requirements, it must be flexible and capable of being extended.

7. It must be able to compute unit performance indices using online real time data.

8. It must be reliable.

These are two types of data acquisition system:

1. Single channel DAS

2. Multi channel DAS

4.3. Single channel DAS:

A single channel data acquisition system consist a signal conditioner followed by A to D converter which performing repetitive conversion at a free running, internally determined rate. The output is in digital codeword including over range indication, polarity information and a status output to indicate when the output digits are valid. A single channel DAS as shown in following figure.

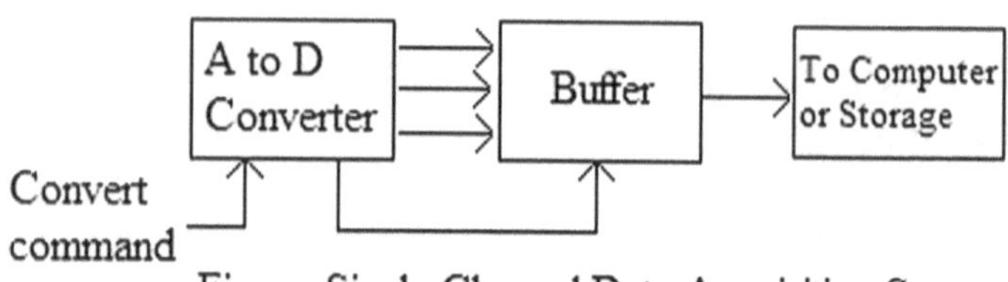

Figure: Single Channel Data Acquisition System

The digital outputs are further fed to storage or print out device or to a digital computer device or to a digital computer for analysis.

4.4. Multichannel DAS:

The number of sub-system of data acquisition system can be divided by two or more input sources. The following figure shows the multi-channel analog multiplexed data acquisition system. It has a single analog to digital convertor. This analog to digital convertor has an input which is selected from multiplexer. The individual analog signals are applied directly or after amplification and or signal conditioning, whenever necessary to multiplexer. As all the data which have to be acquired, originate from different sources so signal conditioning in some cases is required. A simple attenuator is used to down the input gains. Analog differentiation, precision rectification and averaging, phase detection, logarithmic conversion, ratio computations using dividers and many other types of processors are used before DAS. These are further converted to digital signal by using analog to digital convertor. For most efficient utilization of time, multiplexer is made to seek the next channel to be converted while the previous data stored in sample is converted to digital form.

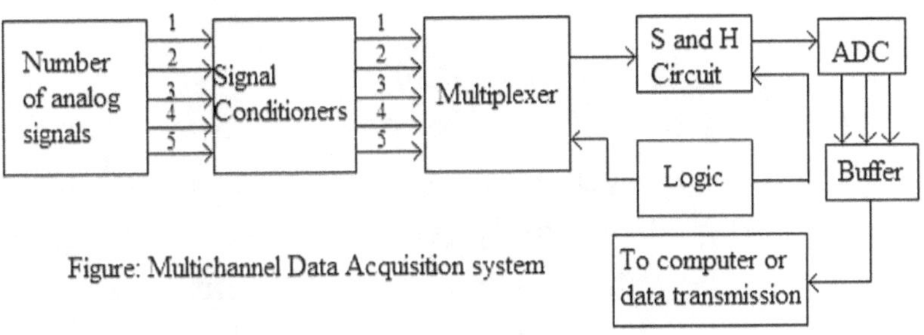

Figure: Multichannel Data Acquisition system

When conversion is complete the status line from convertor causes the sample and holds circuit to return to sample mode and acquires the signal of next channel, on completion of acquisition either immediately. The Sample and hold circuit is switched to hold mode a conversion begins and multiplexer selected the channel.

This method is relatively slower than system, where sample and hold outputs on even A to D convertor output are multiplexed, but it has the obvious advantage of low cost due to sharing of a majority of sub-systems. Sufficient accuracy in measurement can be achieved without the sample and hold, in case where signal amplification is extremely slow. [2, 3]

4.5. Application of DAS:

1. The Data Acquisition system (DAS) is used for collecting the information

2. The DAS can convert the data into usable form.

3. The DAS is used to generate information for display.

4. The DAS is used in industrial process control system.

5. The DAS is used in aircraft control system.

4.6. Converters:

It is necessary to study the basic techniques and circuits employed to convert an analog signal to digital form (analog-to-digital or simply A/D conversion) and those used to convert a digital signal to analog form (digital-to-analog or simply D/A conversion).

4.6.1. D to A converter:

At the output of digital controller the digital signals must be converted into an analog signal by the process called as digital to analog conversion. A digital to analog converter is a device that transforms digital inputs (binary numbers) to an analog output. The Resistor ladder networks provide a simple, inexpensive way to perform digital to analog conversion (DAC). The most popular networks are the binary weighted ladder and the R to 2R ladder. Both these devices will convert digital voltage information to analog. The R- 2R ladder network has become the most popular due to the network's inherent accuracy, superiority and ease of manufacture. Figure 1 is a diagram of the basic R/2R ladder network with N bits. The "ladder" portrayal comes from the ladder-like topology of the network. Note that the network consists of only two resistor values; R and 2R (twice the value of R) no matter how many bits make up the ladder. The particular value of R is not critical to the function of the R/2R ladder. The binary weighted ladder shown in Figure 2 requires double multiples of R as the number of bits increase. As the ratios of the resistors become more and more obtuse in a binary weighted network, the ability to trim the resistors to accurate ratio tolerances becomes diminished. More accurate ratios can be obtained in a resistor network with consistent, similar values as in the R/2R network. The R/2R network provides the most accurate method of digital to analog conversion. [4, 5, 6, 7]

4.6.1.1. Binary weighted network:

The resistive divider network use to change possible states of digital signals into equivalent analog voltages the smallest number represented by 'OOO' is 'O' V while the largest number 111 is 7 i.e. there are 7 discrete levels to be defined. The LSB is given a binary equivalent weight of 1/7 or 1 part in seven MSB is 4/7 or 4 times LSB therefore the total sum of the weight must be equal to,

$$1/7 + 2/7 + 4/7 = 1$$

In general, the binary equivalent weight assign to LSB is $1/2^{n}-1$ where 'n' is the number of bits. A resistive divider network of 'n' number of digital inputs and analog output is as shown in following figure.

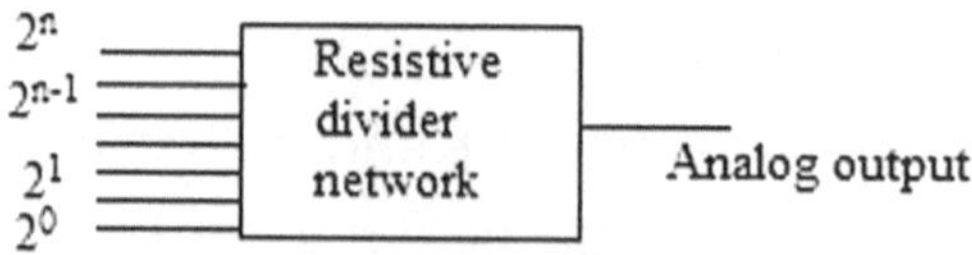

For 3 bit case, assume digital levels O = OV and 1 = 7V. For an input of 001, output is +1V, for 010 it is 2V for 100 it is 4V. The digital inputs like 011 are seen to be combination of 010 and 001. Similarly other levels are determined by an additive of voltage as shown in following table.

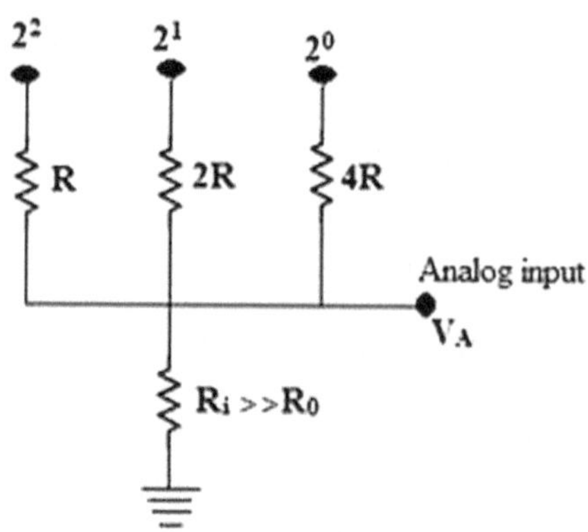

The resistor R, 2R and 4R forms the divider network as shown in above figure. RL is the load to which the divider is connected and is large enough to the load divider network.

Decimal input	Analog output
000	0
001	1
010	2
011	3

For example digital input signal 001 is applied to the network using the levels as before; the equivalent circuit is as shown in following figure.

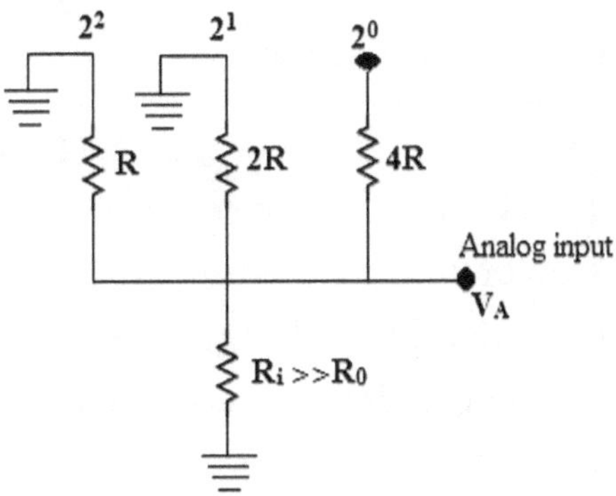

The analog output voltage can be determined by the use of millimen's theorem. The theorem states that the voltage appearing at any node in a resistive network is equal to the summation of the current entering the node divided by the summation of the conductance connected to the load.

It can be given in the equation form as, Applying this theorem to the above figure, it gives,

$$V = \frac{\dfrac{E_1}{R_1} + \dfrac{E_2}{R_2} + \dfrac{E_3}{R_3}}{\dfrac{1}{R_1} + \dfrac{1}{R_2} + \dfrac{1}{R_3}}$$

$$V_A = \frac{\dfrac{V_0}{4R} + \dfrac{V_1}{2R} + \dfrac{V_2}{R}}{\dfrac{4}{4R} + \dfrac{2}{4R} + \dfrac{1}{4R}} = \frac{7}{7} = 1$$

The only drawback of this type of device is that it requires resistors of different values and the resistors should be precision.

4.6.1.2. R/2R Ladder Networks:

An alternative to the binary-weighted-input digital to analog converter is R- 2R ladder network. This D to A converter uses fewer unique resistor values. A disadvantage of the binary weighted DAC design was its requirement of several different precise input resistor values, one unique value per binary input bit.

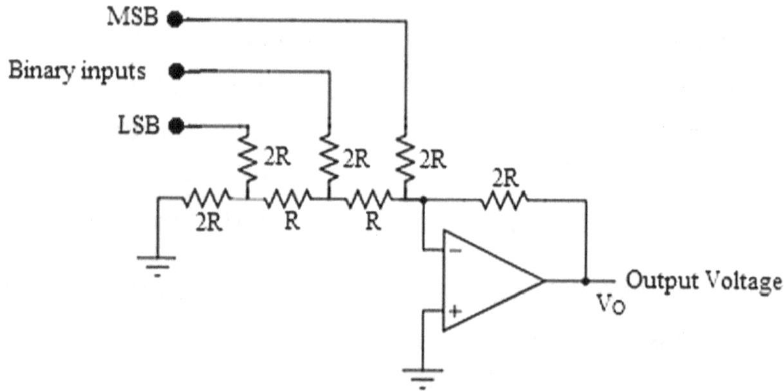

Figure: R-2R ladder A to D converter

R- 2R ladder networks provide a simple means to convert digital information into an analog output. This network provides a simple, inexpensive way to perform D to A conversion. The above figure is the basic of R-2R ladder network with N-bits. The ladder picture comes from the ladder like network. The network consists of only two resistor values R and 2R. No matter that how many bits make up the ladder. The particular values of R are not critical to the function of R- 2R ladder. [8]

A string of (many often) equally dimension resistors connected between two reference voltages. It is a resistors string ladder network in which the resistors act as voltage dividers between the references voltages.

As shown in the following figure, bit 1 is MSB, where as bit N is the LSB. Here MSB means 'a_{N-1}' where as LSB 'a_o' are driven from digital logic gates. Ideally the bits are switched between 'O' V (logic O) and 'V' reference (Logic 1). The R-2R network causes the digital bits to be weighted in their contribution to their output voltage.

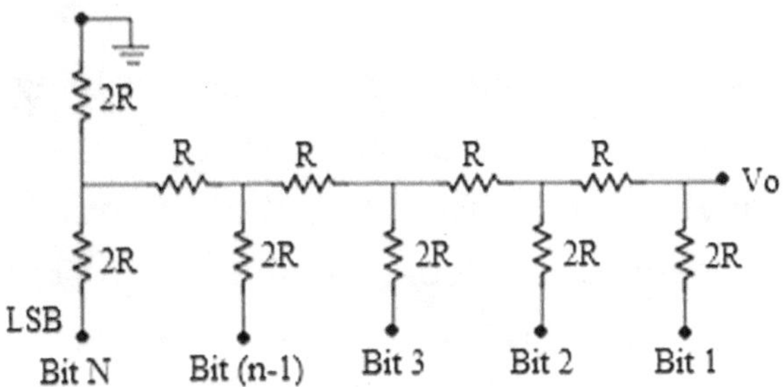

Figure: R-2R ladder network of N-Bits

For example, the circuits have 5 bits therefore its bits are 4 to 0 giving 25 or 32 possible analog voltages at the output. Depending on which bit are set to '1' and to '0', the output voltage will be a corresponding step value between 'O' V and the actual value of V reference. For a digital value (VAL) of R - 2R ladder of N bits, the output voltage Vout is given as,

$$V_{out} = V_{ref} \times VAL/2^N$$

Here, N = 5, Therefore, $2^N = 2^5 = 32$.

With V_{Ref} = 3.3 V, V_{out} will vary between '00000' to '11111'. i.e. VAL = 32.

Minimum single step, VAL = 1.

Therefore, V_{out} = 3.3 X 1/32 = 0.1 V

Maximum output, VAL = 11111 i.e.31.

Therefore, V_{out} = 3.3 X 31/32 = 3.2.V.

The R-2R ladder is inexpensive and relatively easy to manufacture. Since only two resistor values are required. It is fast and has fixed output impedances R.

Although simple in design and function, applying an R- 2R resistor network to a real application requires attention to how the device is specified. Output errors due to resistor tolerances are often overlooked in the design of the digital to analog conversion (DAC) circuit and in the selection of the R/2R ladder itself. This application note identifies these issues, provides methods for calculating R- 2R resolution and accuracy and a means to better specify R- 2R ladder networks. [9, 10]

4.6.2. Analog to Digital converters:

In the real world, the most of the data is characterized by analog signals. In order to manipulate the data using a microprocessor, it is necessary to convert the analog signals in to the digital signals, so that the microprocessor can be able to read, understand and manipulate the data.

The main goal of Analog to Digital Converter is to digitize the analog signals, which means to record and store the analog signals in numbers. The two parameters which control in converting the analog signals to the digital signals are the sampling rate which controls the number of samples taken in a second and sampling precision which controls the number of different gradations (quantization levels) for the sampling process.

4.6.2.1. Successive approximation Analog to Digital converter:

The Successive approximation Analog to Digital conversion is capable of both high resolution as well as high speed. Each conversion is independent of the previous ones and the conversion time is constant and is independent of the magnitude of input voltage.

The converter proceeds to convert analog input by finding a 'yes' or 'no' answer for the following sequence of questions.

1. Is the input greater than one half the whole scales?

2. Is the input greater than one fourth of the full scale?

3. Is the input greater than $3/4^{th}$ the full scale?

The answer to (1) is 'no' then check (ii) If yes then checks for (iii). The process is continued until the desired solution is obtained. The following figure shows schematic diagram of this type of Successive approximation A to D converter. [11, 12]

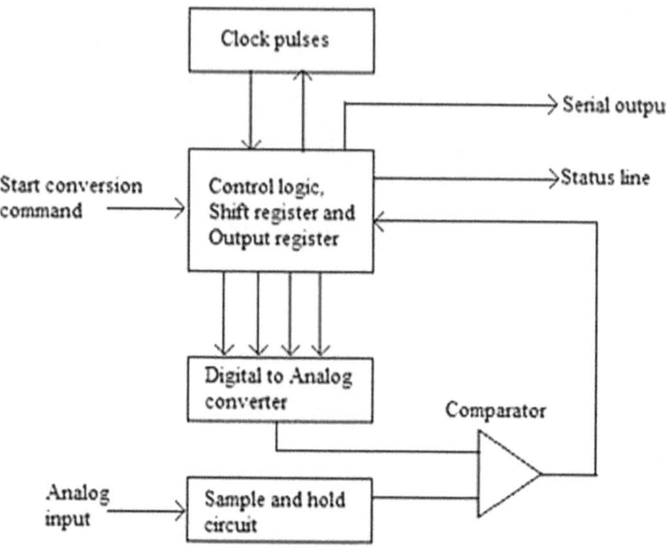

As shown in following figure, initially shift register is clear and on a start command a '1' is stored in MSB. The resulting D to A converter output with the analog input depending on the decision of comparator. The output is 1, if analog input is greater than D to A convertor and otherwise zeros '0'. A one '1' or zero '0' is assigned to MSB or '1' is stored in the next lower bit. Again D to A converter output is compare with the analog input and the earlier process is continued. After the last bit has been tried the status line changes state to indicate the contents of the output register. Now constitute the valid output of conversion process. A digital binary code corresponding to the input signal is thus available at the output. [13]

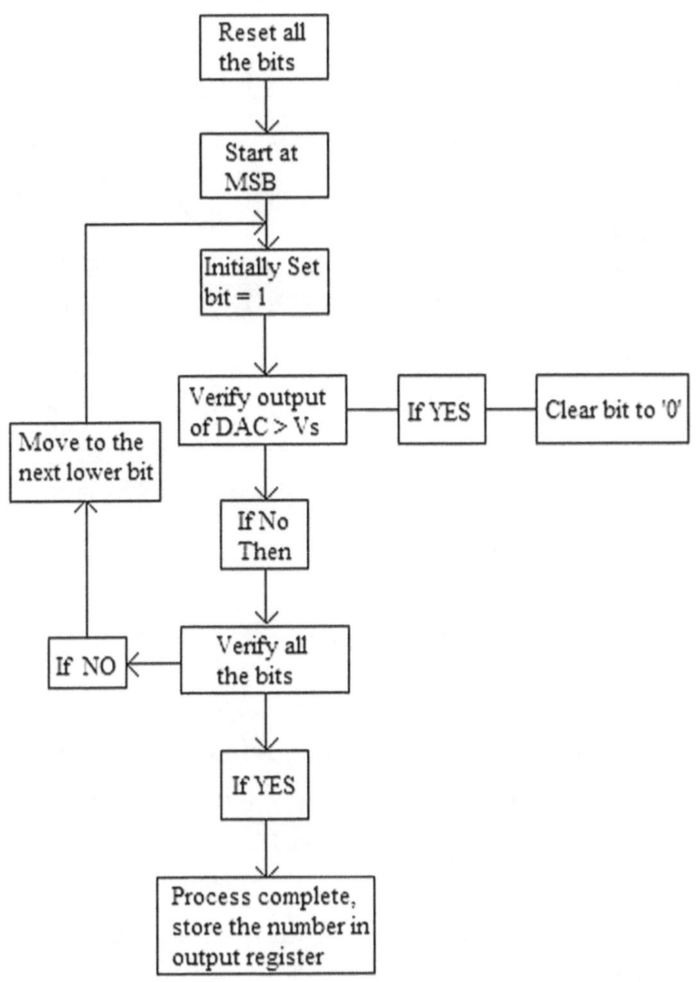

For example, as shown in following figure, 1000 representing the full reference voltage E_r, is divided in to half, (½) gives 0100 to corresponding voltage ½ E_r. A comparison of reference voltage ½ E_r and analog voltage is made, if the result of this comparison shows that, 1st approximation is too small (i.e. ½ E_r < analog input), the next comparison is made against the ¼ E_r, hence after four successive approximations the digital number is stored.

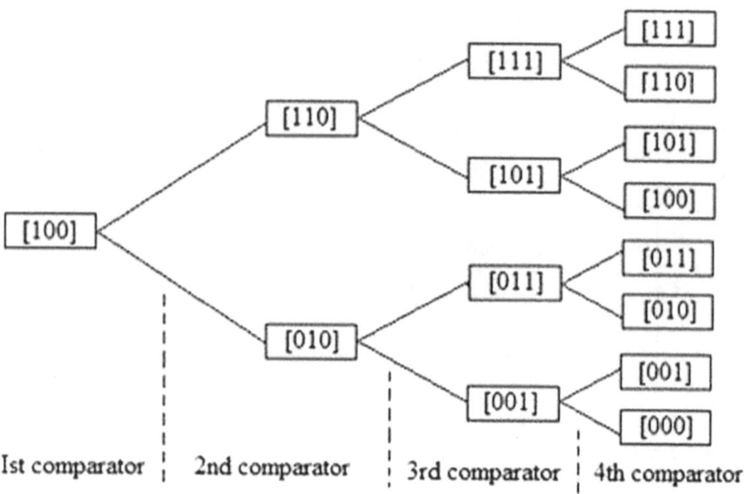

Figure: Successive approxiamation A to D converter

4.6.2.2. Single slope A/D convertor:

In the single slope A to D converter, the ramp output generates the voltage which is equivalent to input. When the voltage generated by ramp is equal to input, the comparator gives output equal to '0'. So the clock pulses to counter are stopped and the counter displays the voltage equivalent to the counts. For example, suppose that if 1 count is equal to 0.1 V. Then 10 counts are 1V. Here 0.1 volt is the minimum voltage the converter can sense.

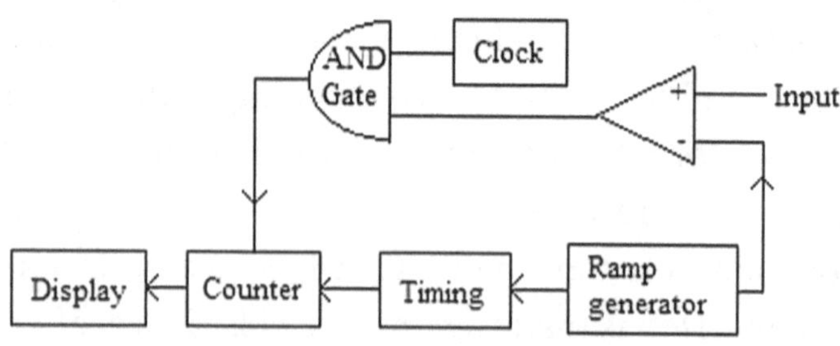

Figure: Single slope A to D converter

The Single slope convertor consist the components are comparator, the constant current source for external capacitor and the free running timer. A conversion begins by the external capacitor discharging through the ground path. The analog single to be converted either is held on the input continuously or is sampled on the internal storage capacitor for the duration of conversion. The current source is used to charge the external capacitor. The charge transferred from the current source to the capacitor results in an increase in the capacitor voltage which causes the comparator to transition from low to high when it reaches the level of sampled analog voltage. The transition of comparator is use to capture the value of the free running timer which is digital representation of the sample voltage.

In the Single slope A to D convertor, current is transfer of charge in a given period of time and is represented as, $I = dq/dt$. In case of capacitor, the charge on the capacitor is proportional to the voltage across it.

i.e. $q = CV$.

$I = d/dt\,(CV)$

i.e. $I = C\,dv/dt$

i.e. $dv = 1/C\,I.dt$.

Integrating the above equation, we get,

$V = 1/C \int I.dt$

For the integration of voltage, the beginning and end of the integral represents the beginning and end of

A to D conversion sequence from the discharge of external capacitor to the time that the comparator transition from low to high. This equation explains why the external capacitor is referred to as an integration capacitor due to the time integration of the current being to source to the external capacitor.

The accuracy of this method is dependent on the tolerance of the passive elements (resistors and capacitors) which varies with the environment, resulting in low measurement repeatability. [14]

4.6.2.3. Dual Slope A/D converters:

The dual slope Analog to Digital converter overcomes the difficulties of the single slope A to D converter method. The basic idea of the dual slope converter is to generates pulse width proportional to V_{in} (i.e. tx < V_{in}) by making a time Comparison between two integrators. [15]

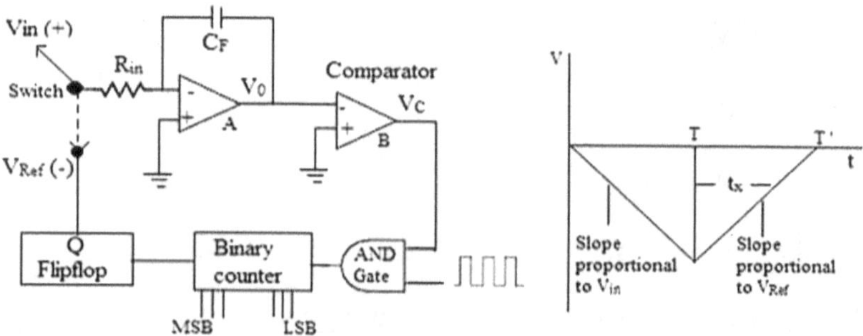

The dual slope A/D converter consists operational amplifier, comparator, binary counter, AND gate, flipflop and the switch. The above figure depicts the circuit diagram for dual slope A/D converter. As shown in the figure, A is the operational amplifier used as an integrator with the input resistor 'R_{in}' and feedback capacitor 'C_f'. The switch used permits the integrator to be connected to the input analog signal voltage or the reference voltage of the opposite polarity. To change the position of the switch the flip-flop acts as a switch driver. When the switch is in the '0' position, i.e. at t = 0, the conversion process starts therefore input analog voltage 'V'_{in}' is connected to the integrator. The integrator proceeds at a slow rate proportional to 'V'_{in}' for a time T and at the end of 't' seconds, the output voltage 'V_0' of the integrator is given by,

$$V_0 = -1/R_{in}C_f \int_0^T V_{in} \, dt,$$

i.e. $V_0 = [-1/R_{in}C_f] V_{in} T + C_1$

Where 'C_1' is the constant of integration.

At, $V_{in} = 0$, $V_0 = 0$ Therefore, $V_0 = - V_{in}.T/R_{in} . C_f$

For the comparator this 'V'_0' is used as one of the input to the comparator. As per the above equation, V_0 is negative ($V_0 < O$) therefore, the output of the comparator i.e. V_c is high. Hence both the inputs of the AND gate are high so the AND gate is enable and the clock pulses can reach the clock input of the counter. The input terminals of the counter which counts from (000) to (111). When $2^n - 1$ clock pulses are applied (where n is number of bits), after the next clock pulse '2^n' at time 't_1' the counter cleared, $T = 2^n T_c$, where period of clock is 'T_c' is and it becomes 1, the counter resets. The switch now moves to position '1' at time 't' and hence connecting to the input of integrator,

$-V_{ref}$. Since V_{ref} is negative, drives the second integrator, the output V_0 of the integrator moves in the positive direction. The above figure shows the timing diagram, which shows, until $V_0 < O$, $V_c = 1$ and the counter continuous to count and as the 'V'$_0$ goes positive at t, V_c becomes low, disabling the AND gate. Therefore the counter stops counting.

Let us suppose that, the counter has recorded 'n' number of counts then $t' -T = t_x = n.T_c$. When the switch is in position '1', the output voltage V_0 of the integrator is given as follows. [16]

$$V_0 = \frac{-V_{in}.T}{R_{in}.C_f} - \frac{1}{R_{in}.C_f} \int_T^t -V_{Ref}\, dt$$

References

1. www.slideshare.net/sumeetpatel21/data-acquisition-system-40835631.

2. Electronic instrumentation by H.S.Kalsi.

3. Instrumentation: Devices and systems by C.S.Rangan, Sharma and Mani.

4. http://global.oup.com/us/companion.websites/9780195323030/student/pdf/

5. DataConverters.pdfhttp://hyperphysics.phyastr.gsu.edu/hbase/electronic/dac.html3.

6. D to A converters https://en.wikipedia.org/wiki/Digital-to-analog_converter.

7. http://global.oup.com/us/companion. websites/9780195323030/student/pdf.

8. http://www.learningelectronics.net/vol_4/chpt_13/3.html

9. DataConverters.pdf   https://en.wikipedia.org/wiki/Resistor_ladder.

10. http://hyperphysics.phy-astr.gsu.edu/hbase/electronic/adc.html.

11. https://en.wikipedia.org/wiki/Analog-to-digital_converter

12. http://laris.fesb.hr/digitalno_vodjenje/download/experiment9.

13. www.learn-c.com/experiment9.

14. www.discuss-book.com/booknote/NDc%3D/Analog-to-Digital-Single-Slope-ADC.

15. http://pe2bz.philpem.me.uk/Lights/-%20Laser/Info-902-LaserCourse/c04-

16. Dual-SlopeConverters,http://pe2bz.philpem.me.uk/Lights/-%20Laser/Info-902-LaserCourse/c04-09/mod04_09.htm

5. Input Output Devices

5.1. Introduction:

It is often necessary to have a permanent record on the state of phenomenon being investigated. In many of industrial and research processes it is necessary to monitor continuously the condition, state or value of process variables such as flow, force, pressure, temperature, current, voltage, power etc. The recorder records the electrical and non-electrical quantity as a function of time. The recording method should be consistent with the type of system. There are two types of recording devices, Analog recorders and Digital recorders.

Analog recorders can be broadly classified into

1.　　Graphic recorders
2.　　Oscillographic recorders
3.　　Magnetic tape recorders

5.2. Graphic recorders:

As the name suggest this type of recorder store or shows the information in graphical manner. A strip chart recorder, XY recorders are the good examples of graphical recorders.

5.2.1. Strip chart recorder:

A strip chart recorder is an electronic instrument that keeps track of various measurements required in industrial as well as laboratory environments. It is used to record the process measurements for the variables such as temperature, pressure, flow, pH, and humidity etc. It is also used in the scientific and engineering fields for testing and diagnostics. In medical field it is vastly used for the diagnosis of the patient.

Strip chart recorder records one more variables with respect to time and so it is also called as x-t recorder. Strip chart recorders consist of a roll or strip of paper that passes linearly below one or more pens. As per the signal variations each pen's deflection records the process being measured. Well suited to recording of continuous processes, strip chart recorders are commonly used in both laboratory and process-measurement applications.

Following figure shows basic constructional features of strip chart recorder. [1]

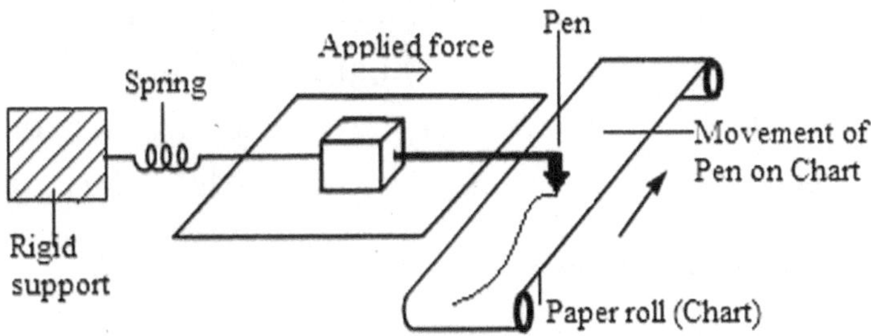

Figure: Construction of Strip Chart Recorder

The strip chart recorder consists of a long roll of graph paper moving vertically. A system for driving the paper at some selected speed. A stylus is used to making marks on the moving graph paper. The stylus moves horizontally in proportional to the quantity being recorded. A stylus driving system moves the stylus in nearly exact replica or analog quantity being recorded. A range selector switch is used so that input to the recorder drives system is within the acceptable level. Most of the recorder used a pointer attached to the stylus. This pointer moves over a calibrated scale thus showing the instantaneous value of the quantity being recorded and external control circuit for the stylus may be used.

In strip chart recorders usually self balancing potentiometers are used. These self balancing potentiometers plot the electro motive force (EMF) as a function of time. The strip chart recorder consist a paper drive system, there are different paper drive system which are discussed below.

Paper drive system:

In this method the position of pen is constant. The paper should move in the uniform speed. For this purpose a spring wound mechanism may be used, means the spring release slowly with the particular constant speed. In most of the recorders a synchronous motor is used to drive the paper.

Marking mechanism:

There are many mechanism used for marking marks on the paper. The most commonly mechanisms are discussed below.

Marking with ink filled stylus:

A stylus used may be of ink filled or of heated tip. A stylus filled with ink works on the principle of gravity or of capillary actions. This requires that the pointer shall support an ink reservoir. Generally red ink is used. The stylus moving over the paper with preprinted scales traces the variation of input signal. This method is most commonly employed as ordinary paper can be used and therefore its cost is also low. The disadvantage of this method is, due to little friction between stylus tip and paper ink splatters at high speed.

Marking with heated stylus:

The tip is used at the end, which will move on the paper, of the stylus can be heated by some means. The heated stylus melts a thin white wax like coating on a black paper base. This method requires a special type of paper. Since the paper required is a special one its cost is high. This method overcomes the difficulties introduced in ink writing systems.

Electric stylus marking:

In electric stylus marking system a paper with a special coating is used. This paper is very sensitive to a current, when current is conducted from the stylus to a paper; there appears a stress on the paper. The only disadvantage of this method is the cost of the paper in very high, due to a special coating paper.

Electrostatic stylus:

This method uses a stylus which produces a high voltage discharge so that it produces a permanent stress on an electro sensitive paper.

Optical marking method:

In this technique photo sensitive paper is used. Here a beam of light is used to write on a photo sensitive paper. Thus this method allows higher frequency to be recorded and permits a relatively large charge speed with good resolution. This technique is also required photo sensitive paper so that its high cost is the drawback. As the writing process is photographic, the paper must be developed before a record is available. So that the technique is not suitable for process where there is a instantaneous monitoring.

Tracing system

There are two types of tracing system used for producing graphic representation.

Curvilinear System:

In this system the stylus is mounted on a central pivot and moves through an arc which allows full width change marking. If the stylus makes a full range recording the line drawn across the chart will be the curve. The time internal will be along this curve segments. The only disadvantage of this of tracing system is due to curved time base lines, charts are very difficult to analysis.

Rectilinear System:

In rectilinear system of graphical representation the stylus is activated by a drive cord to produce the forward and reverse motion as determined by drive mechanism. This system is called as rectilinear system because the stylus produces straight line across a width of a graph/chart. This system is usually used with thermal or electric writing. [2]

5.2.2. XY recorder:

These recorders accept two inputs (X-input and Y-input) and create a chart or graph that displays the activity of one set of data against another. They are useful for determining relationships between the two inputs; for example, an XY recorder might be used in a chemical process to monitor the effect of temperature on pressure.

An X-Y Recorder is an instrument which gives a graphic record of the relationship between two variables. In this recorder an electromotive force (EMF) is plotted as a function of another electromotive force (EMF). This is done by one self balancing potentiometer which controls the position of chart rolls or paper while another sell balancing potentiometer controls the position of recording pen/ stylus. Here EMF used for operation is not a voltage only but it may be output of transducer, which may be measure of force, displacement pressure or any other physical quantity. The following figure depicts the tentative idea regarding XY recorder. [3, 4]

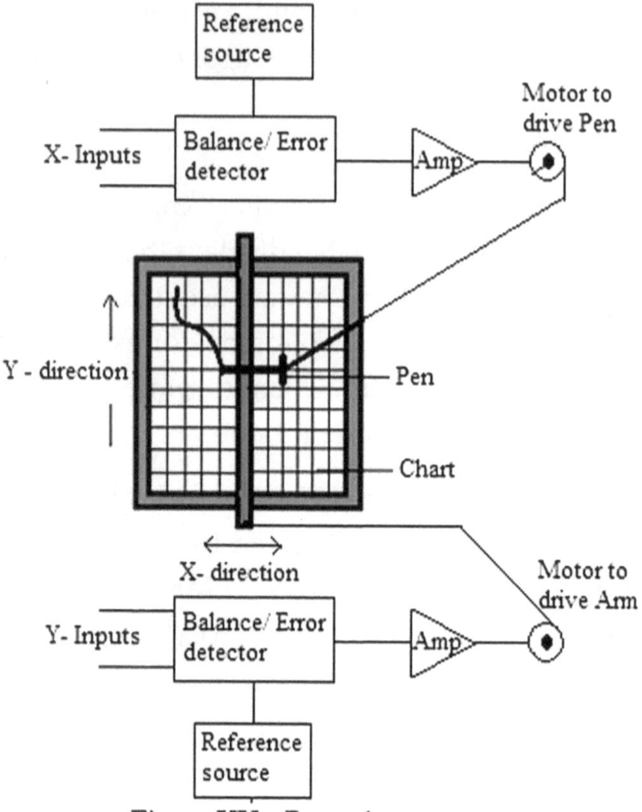

Figure: XY - Recorder

As shown in above figure a signal enters in each of the two channels. The signals are attenuated to the full scale range recorder (say 0.5mV). This signal then passes to a balance circuit, where it will be compare with an internal voltage. The difference between the input signal voltage and the reference voltage, called as error signal is fed to the chopper circuit. The function of chopper circuit is to convert DC signal into AC. The signal is then amplified by servo amplifier in order to activate a servo motor which is used to balance the system and hold it in balance. The action described above takes place in both axes simultaneously thus one can get a record of one variable with respect to another. The instantaneous relationship between two physical quantities, may be electrical or non-electrical can be recorded.

A XY recorder may have a sensitivity of 10 microvolt per mm and frequency response about 6 Hz for both axes. A slewing speed of 1.5 m/sec. The chart side is 250/180 mm the accuracy of x-y recorder is about ± 0.3%.

XY recorders are mainly used to plot resistance temperature characteristics of different materials. To plot stress - strain curve, to plot hysteresis loop etc. Speed – torque characteristics of motor. In laboratories, for many measurements XY recorders are used. [5, 6, 7]

5.3. Paperless Recorders:

Paperless recorders also called as video graphic recorders. These recorders display their charts on an integrated screen. Day to day we experience that, display technology has continually improved with sharpness and color quality. Now a day's move towards the newer advanced PCs. The digital data can usually be stored locally on a disk or card, either of which can be removed for downloading to a PC. A researcher can then bring up any of the stored information for review and analysis, zooming in, during the process disappointment. Where there is conservation of paper, the easy data recovery and sharing of the data are the important benefits. Paperless recorders are the graphical method of choice.

Undoubtedly the traditional chart recorders are forever popular but then again many users tried and true output is so easy to handle, read, and interpret that they wouldn't dream of switching to paperless technology.

5.4. Magnetic recorders:

In 1900, the Poulsen was first demonstrated the principle of magnetic recording. Method of preserving sounds, pictures, and data in the form of electrical signals through the selective magnetization of portions of a magnetic material. Magnetic tape recorders can be used for Data recording and analysis on missiles, aircraft and satellites.

It is frequently describable and in many cases necessary to record data in such a way that they can be reproduces in electrical form again. The magnetic tape recording is the most common and most useful way of achieving this. These recorders have response characteristics which enable then to be used at higher frequency and so these are extensively used in instrumentation systems.

Magnetic tape provides a compact, economical means of preserving and reproducing different forms of information. The objective of a recording system is to record and preserve information pertaining to measurement at a particular time and also to get an idea of the performance of the unit and to provide the results of the steps which are taken by the operator. We know that, the recordings on the tape can be played back immediately and can be easily erased, allowing the tape to be reused without a loss in quality of recording. Hence due to these reasons, the tape is the most widely used of the various magnetic recording mediums. Magnetic tape consists of a narrow plastic ribbon which is coated with fine particles of iron oxide or other magnetic material.

When there is recording on the tape, an electrical signal passes through a recording head as the tape is drawn past, leaving a magnetic imprint on the tape's surface. When the recorded tape is drawn past the playback or reproducing head, a signal is induced that is the equivalent of the recorded signal. This signal is amplified to the intensity appropriate to the output equipment.

Initially for sound recording magnetic tape was designed. After some years, German engineers developed an audio tape recording machine called as the magneto phone. In late 1960s the prerecorded tapes in the form of cartridges and cassettes for sound systems in homes and automobiles were extensively used.

In 1951, the magnetic tape was introduced as a data-storage medium and hence the first digital computer was prepared for commercial use. Magnetic tape recorders have also been widely used to record measurements directly from laboratory instruments and detection devices carried aboard planetary probes. The readings are converted into electrical signals and recorded on tape, which can be later used by researchers for the detail analysis and comparison of that parameter. The block diagram of magnetic tape recorder is as shown in following figure.

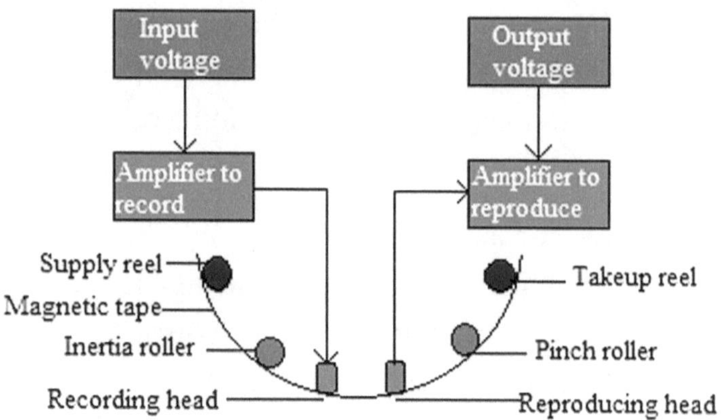

Figure: Magnetic recording system

The magnetic disks are flat circular plates of metal or plastic, coated on both sides with iron oxide. Input signals, which may be audio, video, or data, are recorded on the surface of a disc as magnetic patterns in spiral tracks by a recording head while the disc is rotated by a drive unit. The heads, which are also used to read the magnetic sense on the disc, can be positioned anywhere on the disc with great accuracy. [8]

The Basic Components of magnetic tape Recorder are,

1. Magnetic tape

2. Recording head

3. Reproducing head

4. Supply reel

5. Inertia roller

6. Pinch roller

7. Recording Amplifier and

8. Reproducing amplifier

Recording Head:

The recording head consists of core, coil and a fine air gap of length 5 to 15 micrometer is shunted by passing magnetic tape. This device responds to an electrical signal in such a manner that a magnetic pattern is created in a magnetizable medium. The coil current creates a flux, which passes through the air gap to the magnetic tape and magnetizes the iron oxide particles as they pass the air gap. So the actual recording takes place at the trailing edge of the gap. Any signal recorded on the tape appears as a magnetic pattern dispersed in space along the tape, similar to the original coil current variation with time.

Magnetic Tape:

It is composed of coating of fine magnetic iron oxide particles (Fe_2O_3) on a plastic ribbon. A typical tape size is approximately 1.27 cm wide and thickness is about 2.54 cm. The magnetic particles confirm to the magnetic pattern induce in them and keep them as it is.

Reproducing Head:

This head detects the magnetic pattern stored in them and connects its back to the original electric signal. This head is very similar in appearance to that of recording head.

Tape Transport Mechanism:

Tape transport mechanism moves the tape along the recording or reproducing heads at a constant speed. This must be capable of handling the tape during varies modes of operation with straining, distorting or baring the tape. This requires that the mechanism must use to guide the tape past. The magnetic head with great precision maintain proper tension and obtain sufficient tape to magnetic head contact. An arrangement for fast winding and reversing are also provided. An inertia roller and pinch roller are used to drive the tape.

Principal of Recording:

When a magnetic tape is passed through a recording head any signal recorded on the tape appears as a magnetic pattern dispersed in space along the tape similar to the original coil current variation with time. The same tape when passed through the reproducing head produces variation in the reluctance of the winding thereby inducing a voltage in the winding depends on the direction of the magnetization and its magnitude on the tape. The induced voltage is proportional to rate of change of flux linkage. Therefore the EMF induced in the winding of reproducing head is proportional to rate of change of the level of the magnetization on the tape.

$$E_{rep} \, \alpha \, N \, \frac{d\Phi}{dt}$$

Where, N is the number of turns of the winding of the reproducing heads. Since the voltage produce to reproducing head is proportional to $d\Phi/dt$, the reproduce head acts as a differentiator.

Advantages:

1. These recorders have wide range of frequency.

2. No time is lost in processing because Immediate availability of the signal.

3. Distortion is Low.

4. Can erase and reuse of the tape whenever required.

5. Can play back or reproduce signal as many times as required without loss of signal.[9, 10, 11]

5.5. Null type recorders:

A null type recorder is instrument in which a motor-driven slide wire in a measuring circuit is continuously adjusted so that the voltage or current to be measured will be balanced against the voltage or current from this circuit; a pen linked to the slide wire makes a graphical record of its position as a function of time. Many recorders operate on the principal of change in it input produce the signal from the sensor or transducer upsets the balance of the measuring circuit of the recorder. As a result of this unbalance and error signal is produce that operates same device which restore over balance or brings the system to null condition. The amount of movement of this balance restoring device is an indication of the magnitude of the error signal and the direction of movement is an indication of the direction of the quantity being measured which is deviated from the normal. The signal from the transducer may take any of the several forms. It may be an AC or DC voltage, AC or DC current or it may be a value of resistance, inductance or capacitance. Therefore recorder must be able to accept the form of the input signals. There are number of null type recorder are potentiometric, bridge balance, LVDT, The principal of operation for all these recorder is same i.e. to obtain null condition. The potentiometric type recorder is a self balancing potentiometer which is apart from the indication n is also capable of permanently recording the values of the voltages as they are being measured. This is done by marking device fitted on the pointer under which moves a motor driven chart for recording. The Bridge Type Recorders are used when the signals to be monitored are due to variation in some electrical parameter of a passive transducer such as variation in resistance which occurs in strain gauges, thermostat and photoconductive cells. LVDT Type Recorder is used when signals to be monitored are noticeable in the form of small displacements. In this recorder LVDTs are used to generate a self-balancing capability.

5.6. Light emitting diode (LED):

Light emitting diode is the most important and very useful display device available in market today to use for many applications in instrumentation. Basically it is a PN junction device which emits light. Tha following figure depicts the construction of LED. When current pass through it in forward direction charge carrier's recombination occurs at a PN junction. As electron crosses from N side and recombined with holes on P side. When recombination takes place the charge carriers gives up energy in the form of heat as well as in terms of light. If the semiconducting material is transparent then light is emitted and the junction is the source of light.

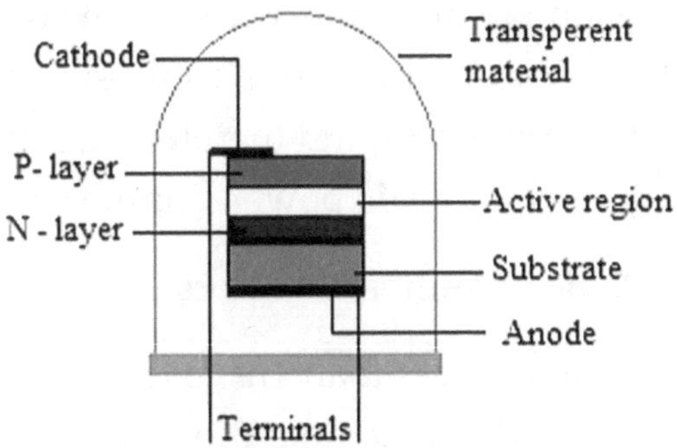

Figure : Construction of LED

For maximum light emission a mental film anode is deposited around the edge of P type material. The cathode connection for the device used usually is gold film at the bottom of N-type region, this helps in reflecting the light to the surface. Gallium Arsenide Phosphate (GaAsP) is a semiconducting material used to emit red or yellow light, Gallium Arsenide (GaAs) emits green red light.

LED are used extensively in segmental and dot matrix displays of numeric and alphanumeric characters. Several LEDs are used in series to form one segment will a single LED may be used to form decimal points. LEDs are available in many colors like green, yellow, red etc. The following fig. shows the cross section of LED. [12]

Advantage:

The Size of LED is tiny so can be stacked together to form numeric and alphanumeric display.

The intensity of light emitted from LED can be smoothly controlled as it is function of current flowing through it.

LED requires moderate power for their operation. A typical voltage drop of 1.2 v and a current of 10mA are required for full brightness and therefore are useful where miniaturization with low dc power is important.

LED are available in number of colors.

The switching time is less than 1ns and therefore they are very useful where dynamic operation of large number of arrays is involved.

LEDs are ragged and can therefore free from shocks and vibration.

LED can be operated in the temperature range of 0°C to 70°C.

Disadvantages:

As compare to LCD, LED required high power.

LEDs are not suited for large area displays, because of their high cost.

5.7. LCD liquid crystal display:

LCD is passive display characterized by very low power consumption and good contrast ratio. The operation of liquid crystal is based on the utilization of a class of organic material which remains regular crystal like crystal even when they have melted. Two liquid crystal materials which are important in display technology are nematic liquid crystal (NLC) and cholesteric liquid crystal as shown in following figure.

The most popular liquid crystal structure is the nematic liquid crystal (NLC). The liquid is normally transparent but if it is subjected to a strong electric field ions moves through it and disturb the well ordered crystal structure causing the liquid to polarized and hence turn the opaque. The removal of applied electric field allows the crystal structure to reform and the material regains its transparency.

Basically the LCD comprises a thin layer of NLC fluid about 10 μm thick sandwiches between two class plates having electrodes, at least one of which should be transparent. If both are transparent then LCD is of Transmission type. Where as a reflective LCD has only one electrode transparent. The structure of typical reflective LCD is as shown in following Figure. The NLC material has a homogenous alignment of molecules while the glass substrate supports the LCD and provides the required transparency. The electrode facilitates the electrical connection for the display. The insulating spaces are the thematic seal. The LCD material is held in the central cell of the glass sandwich the inner surface of which is coated with a very thin conducting layer of tin oxide (SnO_2) which can be either transparent or reflective.[13]

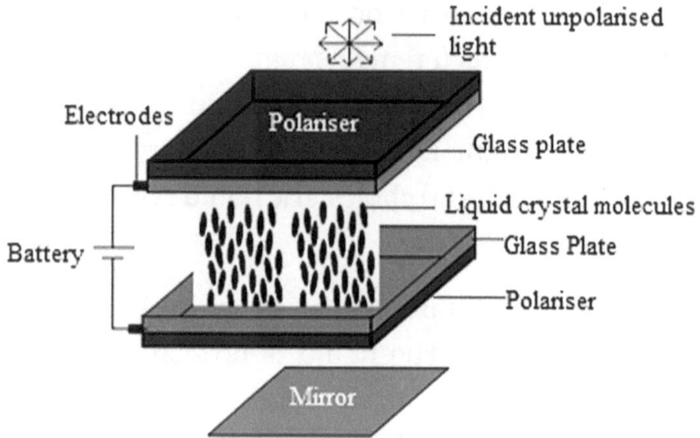

Figure: Liquid Crystal Display, Alignment of liquid crystals when electric field is applied

The oxide coating on the front sheet of an indicator is to produce a single or multi segment pattern of character and each segment of characters is properly insulated from each other.

Important Features:

1. The electric field require to activate LCDs is typically of the order of 104 V/cm. This is equivalent to an LCD terminal voltage of 10 V, when NLC layer is 10μm thick.

2. NLC material possess high resistively i.e. greater than 1010 Ω, therefore the current require for scattering light in an NLC is very marginal (typically 0.1 per cm^2)

3. LCD's are very slow devices; they have turned on time of "few millisecond and turn off time is of 1/10th of millisecond".

Dr. Patil Shriram B.

References

1. www.engr.colostate.edu/~dga/mech307/lectures.

2. http://mediatoget.blogspot.in/2012_04_01_archive.html

3. http://www.ustudy.in/node/3776.

4. A Course in Electrical and Electronic Measurements and Instrumentation by A.K.Sawhney

5. XY recorder, http://mediatoget.blogspot.in/2012_04_01_archive.html.

6. www.allsyllabus.com/aj/note/ECE/ELECTRONIC%20 INSTRUMENTATION/UNIT8/XYrec.

7. XY recorders http://www.ustudy.in/node/3776.

8. http://www.britannica.com/topic/magnetic-recording.

9. http://instrumentationandcontrollers.blogspot.in/2012/06/what-is-magnetic-tape.

10. Instrumentation engineering, By U.K.Bakshi. A.V.bakshi.

11. Electronic instrumentation 3E, By H.S.Kalsi.

12. http://nguyenmarysci4.tumblr.com/post/45739083253/what-the-led-how-it-does.

13. http://education.mrsec.wisc.edu/147.htm.

6. Measurement of temperature

6.1. Introduction:

Temperature is one of those aspects of the everyday world that seems rather conceptual when viewed from the point of view of physics. Scientifically, it is not simply a measure of hot and cold, but is an indicator of molecular motion and energy flow. Thermometers measure temperature by a number of means, including the expansion that takes place in a medium such as mercury or alcohol. These measuring devices are gauged in several different ways, with scales based on the freezing and boiling points of water.

Temperature may be defined as a measure of the average molecular translational energy in a system that is, in any material body. Temperature determines the direction of internal energy flow between two systems when heat is being transferred. This can be illustrated through an experience familiar to everyone: having one's temperature taken with a thermometer. If one has a fever, one's mouth will be warmer than the thermometer, and therefore heat will be transferred to the thermometer from the mouth until the two objects have the same temperature. At that point of thermal equilibrium, a temperature reading can be taken from the thermometer.

6.2. Temperature Scales:

Fahrenheit:

German physicist Daniel Fahrenheit (1686-1736) built the first thermometer to contain mercury as a thermometric medium. Alcohol has a low boiling point, whereas mercury remains fluid at a wide range of temperatures. In addition, it expands and contracts at a very constant rate, and also it does not stick to glass. In addition its silvery color makes a mercury thermometer easy to read.

The Swedish astronomer Anders Celsius (1701-1744) created in 1742 temperature measure in metric scale is the Celsius scale. Like Fahrenheit, Celsius chose the freezing and boiling points of water as the two reference points. Celsius's scale was based not simply on the boiling and freezing points of water, but, also on those points at normal sea-level atmospheric pressure. A Celsius degree is equal to 1/100 of the difference between the freezing and boiling temperatures of water at 1 atm. The Celsius scale is sometimes called as the centigrade scale, as it is divided into 100 degrees, (cent is a Latin word and means "hundred").

In 1787, French physicist J. A. C. Charles (1746-1823) invented a new scale called Kelvin. The Kelvin scale is based not on the freezing point of water, but on absolute zero, the temperature at which molecular motion comes to a practically stop. This is $-273.15°C$ which in the Kelvin scale is designated as 0K(zero Kelvin). In Kelvin scale it is to be noted that, measures do not use the symbol for "degree."

The conversion of temperature scale Celsius into Fahrenheit is as,

$$^\circ F = 32 + \frac{9}{5}\,^\circ C$$

Similarly the relation between Rankin and Kelvin is as,

$$R = \frac{9}{5}\,K$$

There are many types of thermometers. The major ones employ the characteristics of expansion and contraction of substance according to the temperature, employ the valuable of electrical characteristics say, electrical resistance of substance according to temperature, or make use of characteristics between temperature and heat radiation energy emitted from surface of substance.[1,2,3]

6.3. Temperature measurement methods:

There are three different method of temperature measurement.

6.3.1. Non-electrical method:

A change in temperature causes some kind of mechanical motion, typically due to the fact that most material expands with a rise in temperature. Mechanical thermometers can be constructed which use solid, liquid even as even gases as the temperature sensitive material.

The non electrical method based on one of the following principle,

a) Change in physical state

b) Change in chemical properties

c) Change in physical properties

These are devices are used in the areas where there is risk of explosion.[4,5]

6.3.1.1. Liquid in glass thermometer:

In this type of thermometer, it is important that the glass tube should be kept sealed; otherwise, atmospheric pressure contributes to inaccurate readings, because it influences the movement of the thermometric medium. One cannot use water as a liquid, because water quickly proved unreliable, due to its unusual properties, i.e. it does not expand uniformly with a rise in temperature, or contract uniformly with a lowered temperature. Therefore, mercury, alcohol, which responds in a much more uniform manner to changes in temperature, took its place.

6.3.1.2. Mercury thermometer:

The mercury is the most preferred thermometric medium used in thermometers. Alcohol is still used in thermometers today. Alcohol has its advantages include a much higher boiling point, a tendency not to stick to glass, and a silvery color that makes its levels easy to gauge visually. Like alcohol, mercury expands at a uniform rate with an increase in temperature hence, the higher the temperature, the higher the mercury stands in the thermometer.

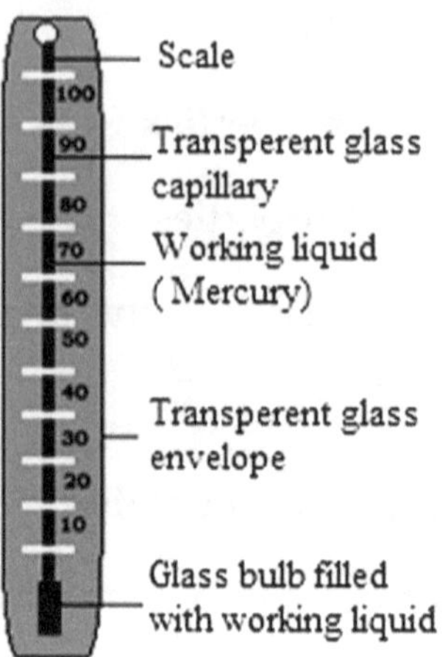

Figure: Liquid in glass thermometer

In a typical mercury thermometer, mercury is placed in a long, narrow sealed tube called a capillary. The capillary is decorated with figures for a calibrated scale. Thermometer is calibrated by measuring the difference in height between mercury at the freezing point of water, and mercury at the boiling point of water. The interval between these two points is then divided into equal increments. [6, 7]

6.3.1.3. Pressure Thermometers:

This type of thermometer based on the principle of fluid expansion. It consists of temperature sensor in the form of sensing bulb. Armoured capillary tube is coupled with the sensing bulb along with the bourdon tube. The force end of the bourdon tube is attached with the mechanical linkage to the movement of indicator which moves on the scale.

As shown in the following figure, the sensing bulb is placed in the proximity of the source whose temperature is to be measure. Because of the thermal radiations the liquid enclosed in the sensing bulb get expands and hence create the change in volume which drives the elastic element through the capillary tube. The indicator coupled with this elastic element through mechanical linkage gets deflected and this deflection is a function of temperature.

The range of this type of thermometer is from -130° to 540°c in the linear range. The accuracy of this device is of the order of 1% at low range i.e. up to 300°c whereas it is 2% above this range. [8]

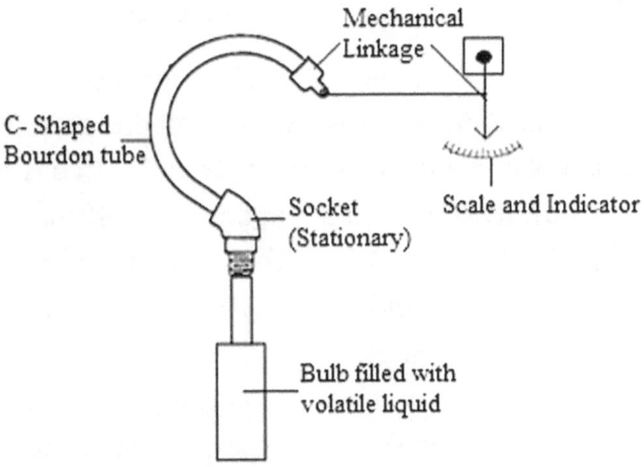

Figure: Constant Volume Thermometer

6.3.1.4. Vapor pressure Thermometer:

The vapor pressure thermometers are very similar in design and construction to that of the constant volume thermometer except the bulb is replaced with an emulsion tube. The emulsion tube is partially filled with low B.P liquid and partially filled with its vapor. Dalton's law of partial pressures states that in a mixture of non-reacting gases, the total pressure exerted is equal to the sum of the partial pressures of the individual gases. In this devices the change in vapor pressure in is a function of temperature and is determined from the vapor pressure curve of that liquid. The liquid used in this device are ethylene, ethyl-either, toluene etc. The major disadvantage of this device is its indication scale is non-linear. However they are widely used for monitoring and controlling in process instrumentation. [9]

6.3.1.5. Bimetallic resistance thermometer:

These types of thermometers employ a principle of solid expansion. The device consists of a bimetallic strip usually in the form of curvilinear beam made up of two different metals. Naturally the thermal expansion coefficient of the two metals is different. When these two form bimetallic strip then the relative motion between them is prevented. When the temperature increases there is deflection of the free end of the strip because of bending of the strip. For example, metal B has smaller expansion coefficient than metal A, as the temperature increases, metal A expands more than the metal B.

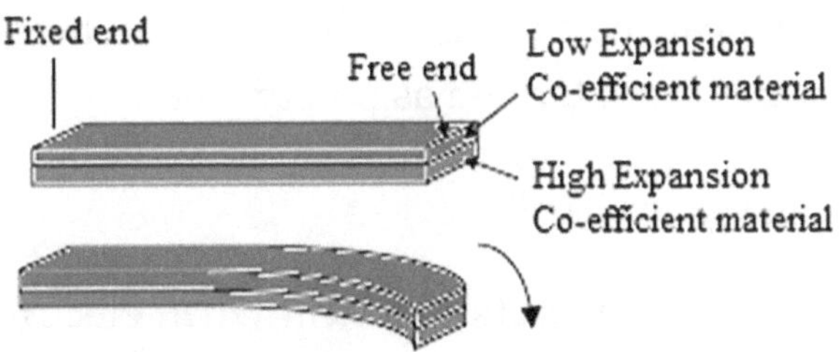

Figure: Bimetallic Strip

A plane bimetallic strip is somewhat insensitive so that a longer strip of a helical form is to be preferred. One end of the helical strip is implemented to the casing, to a source of which temperature is to be measure and the other end of it is connected to the indicator via mechanical linkage which moves over a circular dial graduated in degree of temperature.

It is employed in the range of -30°C to 550°C and accuracy is of the order of 1% (full) whole scale deflection. [10]

6.4.1. Seebeck effect:

Seebeck was the first who was experimentally found that the magnitude of electro motive force, EMF "E" depends on the material as well as the temperature difference. Hence the relation between electromotive force, E and temperature difference, "t_1 and t_2" forms the basis of thermoelectric measurement and is known as Seebeck effect.

6.4.2. Peltier effect:

When thermoelectric current is passed through the two conductors A and B heat may be generated at the cold function or heat may be removed from the hot junction. The phenomena are termed as peltier effect.

6.4.3. Thomson effect:

The absorption or evolution of heat when electric current passes through a circuit composed of a single material that has a temperature difference along its length. This transfer of heat is superimposed on the common production of heat associated with the electrical resistance to currents in conductors.

If a conducting wire, say, copper wire carrying a steady electric current is subjected to external heating at a small part while the rest remains cooler, heat is absorbed from the copper as the conventional current approaches the hot point and heat is transferred to the copper just beyond the hot point. This effect is known as Thomson effect, was discovered by the British physicist William Thomson in 1854.

In short, if a temperature gradient exists along either or both the material the junction electromotive force (emf) may be slightly altered known as Thomson effect. In practical thermoelectric circuits this effect is neglected.

6.4.4. Law of intermediate temperature:

The sum of emf generated by two thermocouples, one with its junction at some temperature say $50°C$ and some reference temperature and the other with its junction at the same reference temperature is equivalent to that of emf produced by single thermocouple with its junction at that 50°C temperature. In general the emf generated in a thermocouple with junctions at temperature T_A and T_C is equal to the sum of emf's generated by similar thermocouples which are acting between T_A and T_B and the other between T_B and T_C, when T_B lies between T_A and T_C.

6.4.5. Law of intermediate metal:

If a thermocouple made up of two metals A and B, when a third metal C is inserted between them, three junctions are formed but there will be no change in thermo electric emf, as the original junction. The maximum accuracy is obtained when leads are of same material.

6.5. Electrical Method:

6.5.1. Thermoelectric transducer:

Thermo electric transducer means thermal to electrical transducer. There are several kinds of thermoelectric transducers. The most common of these is the thermocouple, in which a voltage difference is generated between two dissimilar metals when a temperature difference is applied. This effect has been used for temperature measurement

The most common method of temperature measurement is thermocouple. When two dissimilar metallic wires covering with insulating material twisted or welded together forms two function one is a reference junction i.e. keeping it at the ice bath (0°c) while at the other junction is kept at the source of which temperature is to be measure, forms the thermocouple. When a high resistance voltmeter is connected across it, it reads the electromotive force and which value depends on the material of the wire.

6.5.2. Thermocouple:

Thermocouple is a device which is made up of two dissimilar metals welded or joined together to forms the two junctions. The one junction was keeping at reference temperature say ice bath (0°C) while another is kept at the proximity of the source which temperature is to be measure.

The following factor should take into account when the material can be choice for the construction of the thermocouple.

1) Ability to oppose the temperature at which they are used.

2) The material should free from contamination or oxidation.

3) The characteristic must be linear.

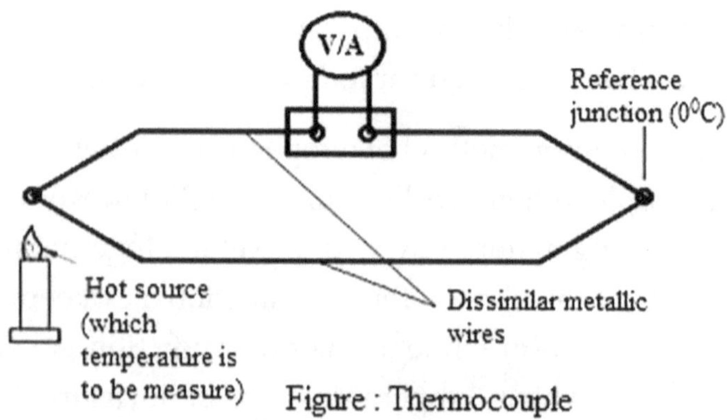

Figure : Thermocouple

The main problem with thermocouple temperature measurement is that, the wires connected to the voltmeter are of the different materials so that, it creates again additional two junctions, which can creates the error when trying to measure the voltage. This error can be overcome by inserting third metal so that same leads can be connected to the voltmeter as shown in the following figure 2. A typical thermoelectric response of Cu-Fe thermocouple is shown in above figure.

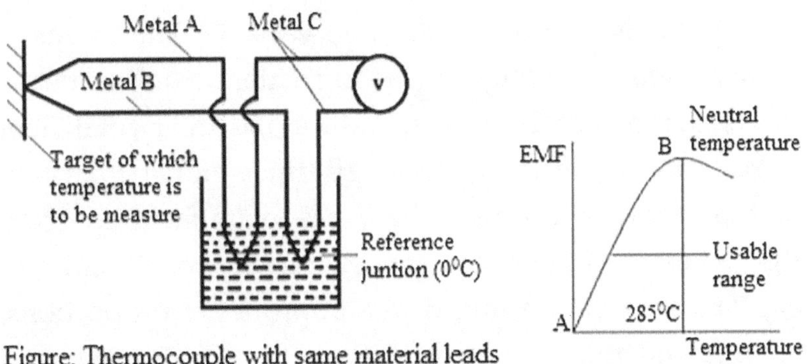

Figure: Thermocouple with same material leads

As shown in graph, It has nearly linear range between A and B which is a useable range of thermocouple, it indicate that as the temperature difference increases the thermocouple EMF 'E' increases reaches to a maximum value i.e. 285°C and then falls so this temperature is called as the neutral temperature.

Thermocouple are broadly classified into two groups

1) Rare metal thermocouple

2) Base metal thermocouple

Rare metals are those which are formed with the combination of rare metals like platinum, tungsten, rhodium, molybdenum etc and their alloys which can be used as temperature sensor up to 290°k.

Base metals are those which are formed with the combination of base metal and their alloys. Their working range is up to 1177°C. [11, 12, 13]

6.5.3. Thermistor (semiconductor resistance sensor):

Thermistor is thermally sensitive variable resister made up of ceramics like semiconducting material, unlike metals thermistor responds to temperature and their coefficient of resistance is of the order of 10 times higher than that of platinum or copper. These are manufactured from the oxide of copper manganese, nickel, cobalt, lithium etc. These oxide are mixed in a appropriate proportions, compressed into desired shapes from powered and applying heat treatment to recrystallize them resulting in a dense ceramic body with the required resistance temperature characteristics. The following figure shows the thermistors of different shapes. [14]

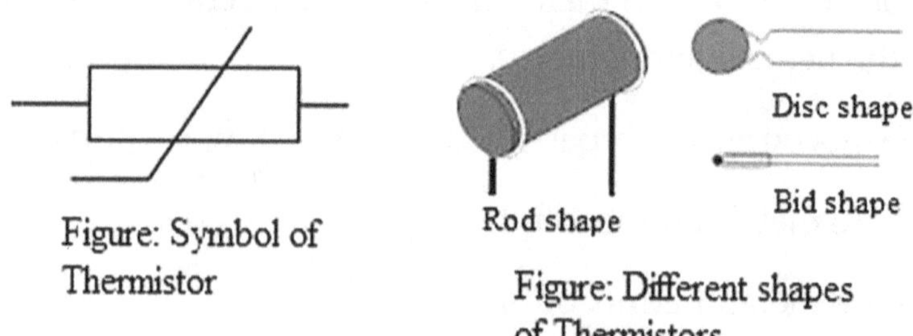

Figure: Symbol of Thermistor

Figure: Different shapes of Thermistors

For the temperature measurement it should have the following characteristic/advantages:

1) Ability to oppose electrical and mechanical stresses.

2) It gives fast speed of thermal response because of high sensitivity & the availability in small sizes.

3) It has good operating range i.e. from 100°c to 300°C.

4) It gives accuracy of 0.01°c with proper calibration.

5) Low cost and easily adaptability to the available resistance bridge circuit.

Drawbacks:

The resistance - temperature characteristic are highly non-linear.

The problem of self heating.

6.5.4. Metallic resistance thermometer:

The metallic resistance thermometer consist the metallic wire wound on the hollow insulating ceramic former and is covered with the protective cement. The ends of the metallic wire are welded to copper leads which are outside then connected to the supporting circuits like the bridge. The total assembly is placed in the medium of which the temperature is to be measure. Metals such as, Platinum, Tungsten, Nickel, etc. possesses positive temperature coefficient (PTC) characteristic and are used up to 600°C with high degree of accuracy.[15]

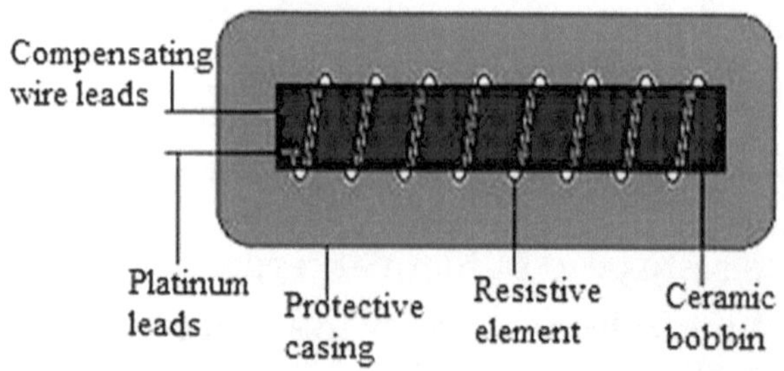

Figure: Metallic resistance thermometer

When the total assembly is placed in the medium of which temperature Is to be measure, the two leads (as shown in figure) are connected to the one of the arms of the bridge circuit. The resistance change due to temperature, unbalance the bridge, which was initially balanced and hence the resistance required to null the balance is used to estimate the temperature coefficient. A protective metal sheath is used to provide the rigidity and mechanical strength. Platinum is the most widely used though it has low sensitivity and high cost as compare to other because-

Over a wide range of temperature, the resistance - temperature characteristics are well defined and stable.

It has high resistance to chemical attack and contamination, ensuring long term stability.

6.6. Radiation method:

The mechanical and electrical methods require a direct physical contact with the body of which the temperature is to be measure. Many a times it is impracticable when one has to measure the higher temperature for example 1000°C. Hence the non contact type devices are required at such places. These devices works on the absorption of heat radiation from certain distance and so such a method of temperature measurement are called as radiation method.

Principle:

The radiations from the source are passes through the objective lens and adjust the detector such that all the radiation concentrates on it. By connecting the moving coil instrument, one can measure the temperature in terms of voltage or current and then this voltage/current can be converted in to temperature scale (as shown in following figure). As these devices measure the higher temperature say fire, these devices are called as pyrometers (Pyro means fire).

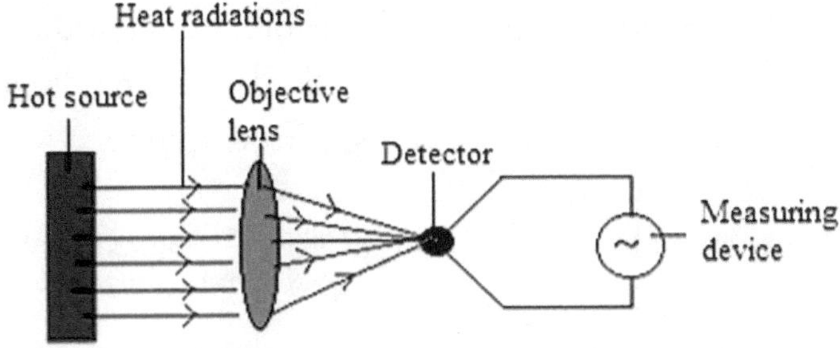

Figure: Working principle of Pyrometers

There are two types of pyrometer

1. Total radiation pyrometer

2. Optical or partial/selective pyrometer

6.6.1. Total radiation pyrometer:

The total radiation means it contains invisible as well as visible rays. A pyrometer is used to measure the temperature of an object from a distance, without making a direct contact. The method used for making these non-contacting temperature measurements is known as radiation pyrometry. Non-contact temperature sensors use the concept of infrared radiant energy to measure the temperature of objects from a distance. After determining the wavelength of the energy being emitted by an object, the sensor can use integrated equations that take into account the source material and surface qualities to determine its temperature.

As shown in following figure, the total radiation pyrometer consist of a blackened tube (not shown in figure) open at one end to receive the heat radiation from the object of which temperature is to be measure. At the other end there may a sighting aperture, attached with an adjustable eye piece, so that researcher can see inside the tube.

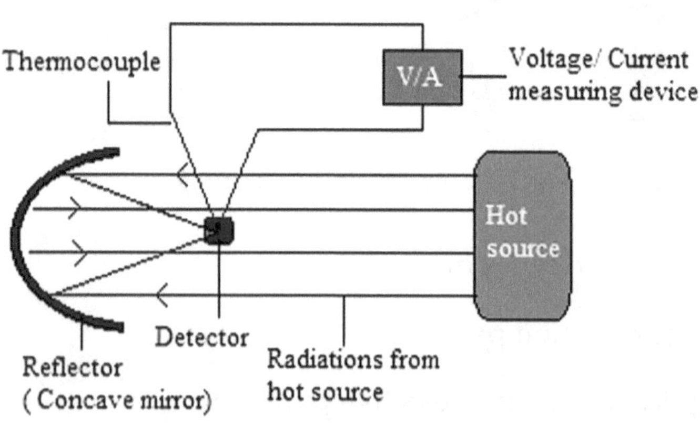

Figure: Experimental arrangement of the Total radiation Pyrometer

Inside the blackened tube concave mirrors are there, so that the thermal radiations incident on the mirror gets reflected and strikes on the detector. By rack and pinion arrangement the proper focusing of thermal radiations will be adjusted on the detector disc. At the disc the thermocouple is connected which is connected to the current/voltage measuring device. This current/voltage is converted into equivalent temperature scale. The shielding element shown is use to protect the detector disc from thermal and mechanical shocks.

The advantage of a radiation pyrometer is there is no need of direct contact with what you are measuring the temperature of. Some drawbacks are,

Though the device is very simple but it is expensive.

The Installation cost is also very high.

The devices are rugged, but do require routine maintenance to keep the sighting path clear, and to keep the optical elements clean.

Pyrometers used for more difficult applications may have more complicated optics, probably rotating or moving parts.

Industries do not accepted calibration curves for pyrometers. [16]

6.6.2. Selective radiation pyrometer:

The principle of the selective radiation pyrometer based on the plank's law, which states that "the energy levels in the radiations from a hot body are distributed in the different wavelengths, as the temperature increases the emissive power shifts to the shorter wavelengths.

The disappearing filament optical pyrometer is one of the classical form of the optical pyrometer. It is most accurate pyrometer of all radiation pyrometers. This radiation pyrometer requires a visual brightness match by a human operator, so that it has limited temperature range, up to 700°C. The following figure is the experimental setup of disappearing filament pyrometer.

As shown in the following figure, an image of target is superimposed on the heated filament. A previously calibrated tungsten lamp which is very stable is used. When the current flows through the filament is known, and then obviously the brightness temperature of the filament is also known.

A red filter passes only a narrow band of wavelengths around 0.65 um = 6500 A0 is placed between the observer eye and the tungsten lamp and the target image.

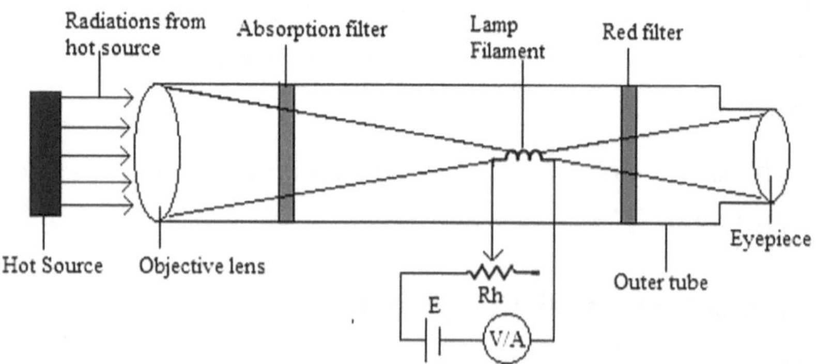

Figure : Tentative construction of Optical Pyrometer

The observer controls the lamp current until the filament disappears in the superimposed target image as shown in following figure. The temperature calibration is made in terms of lamp heating current. Because of the manual null balancing principle this pyrometer is not useable for continuous recording or automatic control application. However it is more accurate and less subject to large errors than the total radiation pyrometers. The accuracy is about ±5°c in the range of 800°C to 1200°C. Accuracy is ±10% when it is used in extended range up to 2000°C. [17, 18, 19]

References

1. http://abyss.uoregon.edu/~js/glossary/temperature_scale.html.

2. https://en.wikipedia.org/wiki/Temperature.

3. http://hyperphysics.phy-astr.gsu.edu/hbase/thermo/temper.html

4. www.nptel.ac.in/courses/108105063/pdf/L04(SS)(IA&C)%20((EE)NPTEL).pdf.

5. Temperature sensors, http://www.electronics-tutorials.ws/io/io_3

6. http://automationwiki.com/index.php/Liquid-In-Glass_Thermometers.

7. www.bipm.org/utils/common/pdf/its-90/TECChapter15.pdf

8. www.globalspec.com/reference/10945/179909/chapter-7-temperaturemeasurement.

9. https://sites.google.com/site/celcius instruments thermometer / types-de thermometer

10. http://instrumentationandcontrollers.blogspot.in/2010/09/bimetallic thermometer.

11. www.marineinsight.com/tech/marine-electrical/thermocouples-the-most-common-

12. www.efunda.com/designstandards/sensors/thermocouples/thmcple_theory.cfm.

13. http://www.pdhonline.org/courses/e166/e166content.pdf

14. www.antonine-education.co.uk

15. www.globalspec.com/reference/10950/179909/chapter-7-temperature-measurement.

16. Total radiation pyrometer, http://slideplayer.com/slide/736420/

17. www.machineryspaces.com/temperature-measurement.

18. http://podelise.ru/docs/49780/index-4626-1.html?page=6.

19. www.instrumentationtoday.com/optical-pyrometer/2011/08/

7. Measurement of pressure

7.1. Introduction:

Pressure is the mechanical concept. Basically, pressure is in the dimensions of mass and length. It is defined as the force per unit area at a given point or surface. In our day to day life, pressure measurements, such as for tire pressure, are usually made relative to ambient air pressure. In other cases measurements are made relative to a vacuum or to some other specific reference. The following terms are used when distinguishing between these zero references.

Absolute pressure: It is the value of pressure above the reference value of perfect vacuum. It is equal to gauge pressure plus atmospheric pressure.

Gauge pressure: It is above the reference value of atmospheric pressure. Atmospheric pressure at sea level is 14.7 lB/in^2 or pound per inch square inch or 1.013×10^{-5} N/m^2 or 760mm of Hg. it is equal to absolute pressure minus atmospheric pressure. Differential pressure is the difference in pressure between two points.

There are number of units used to express the pressure. Some of these derive from a unit of force divided by a unit of area; the   MKS (SI) unit of pressure is the Pascal (Pa). One Pascal is equal to one Newton per square meter. The pound-force per square inch (psi) is the traditional unit of pressure. Pressure is also expressed in terms of standard atmospheric pressure; the atmosphere (atm) is equal to this pressure. The torr is also one of the units of pressure. The manometric units such as the millimeter of mercury (Hg), centimeter of water, and inch of mercury are also used to express pressures in terms of the height of column of a particular fluid in a manometer. Blood pressure is measured in millimeters of mercury. Some of the units of pressure are correlated as follows,

$1 \text{ Pascal} = 1 \text{ N/m}^2. = 9.87 \times 10^{-6}$ atmosphere. $= 7.5 \times 10^{-3}$ Torr.

$1 \text{ Torr} = 1.315789 \times 10^{-3}$ atmosphere $= 1/760$ atmosphere $= 1\text{mm of Hg}$

Static pressure: The pressure exerted at point is identical in all directions. In moving fluid various pressure components may exists in medium. Pressure transducers are classified as:

Gravitational and elastic type: Manometer is a device which is under the head of gravitational type while elastic membranes such as diaphragm, bellow capsules, bourdon tube etc. Sensing diaphragm are made from metal alloys such as bronze, phosphor bronze, beryllium copper, stainless steel or from propriety metal alloys such monel, nickel, ferrous nickel alloy etc. The diaphragm is fabricated, pressing, stamping or spinning from sheets. [1]

Main consideration should take into account while selecting the material of diaphragm is as given below.

- Chemical nature of fluid contact with diaphragm.
- The temperature range required.

- The Effect of shock and vibrations.
- Frequency response requirement.

There are three types of pressure measuring instruments/devices.

7.2. Mechanical instruments:

These instruments may be classified into two groups,

1. Pressure measurement is made by balancing an unknown force with known the forces.

2. Quantitative deformation of an elastic membrane for pressure measurement.

Electromechanical Instruments:

These instruments usually employ the mechanical means for detecting the pressure and electrical means for indicating or recording the detecting pressure.

Electronic instruments

The electronic instruments depend on some physical change that can be detected indicator or recording electronically.

The gas pressure determination is less in magnitude than the atmospheric pressure. This low pressure can be expressed in terms of the height in millimeters of a column of mercury. The height of the column of mercury which the pressure will support may also be expressed in micrometers. Torr is the most commonly used unit and is equal to 1 mm of mercury (Hg).

Pressures above 1 Torr can be easily measured by familiar pressure gages, such as liquid-column gages, diaphragm-pressure gages, bellows gages, etc. Pressures below 1 Torr, mechanical effects such as hysteresis, make these gages impractical.

Pressures below 1 Torr are best measured by gages which infer the pressure from the measurement of some other property of the gas, such as thermal conductivity or ionization. The thermocouple gage, in combination with a hot- or cold-cathode gage (ionization type), is the most widely used method of vacuum measurement today.

The McLeod gage, Pirani gage, and the Knudsen gage are the gages used to measure the vacuum in the range of less than or equal to 1.

7.2.1. Mcload gage:

It is a modified manometer. The principle of which is to compress the known volume of a gas to a higher pressure and measuring the resulting volume change.

The following figure depicts the Mcload gage. As shown in figure, the unknown pressure source of which pressure is to be measure is connected to pressure gauge. Capillary is filled with low pressure gas and the mercury level is so adjusted that the pressure source fills the bulb and capillary, mercury is then force out of the reservoir up in the bulb and reference column 'R'.[2]

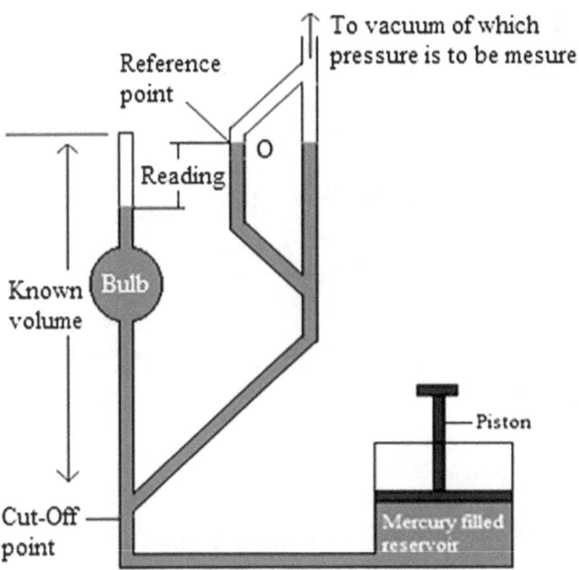

Figure: Construction of Mcload gage

When the levels reaches the cutoff point 'F' a known volume of gas is trapped in the bulb and capillary, the mercury level is raised till it reaches the point 'O' reference point in 'R'. Under this condition the volume remaining in the capillary is read directly from the scale and the difference in height 'Δy' is a measure of the pressure P. It is given as,

$$P = \frac{P_c V_c}{V_f} \text{------------1}$$

Where, Pc is the Pressure of gas in the capillary after compression.

V_c – Volume of gas in the capillary after compression.

$$V_c = A.\Delta y \text{------------2}$$

Where, A – Area of the capillary, V_f – Volume of the gas in capillary and bulb till F.

$$\text{Also,} \quad .\Delta y = Pc - P \text{ ----------3}$$

From equations, 1, 2 and 3 we get,

$$P = \frac{A.\Delta y^2}{V_f - A\Delta y}$$

The capillary can be directly calibrated in terms of pressure P.

7.2.2. Pirani gage:

The rate of heat transfer through a gas is a function of gas pressure after a suitable calibration. The rate of heat transfer can be used as measure of vacuum. At high pressure the heat transfer is by intermolecular collision and collision with the filament takes places and loss of heat has some complex function of pressure. As the pressure continuous to fall, the collision with walls dominant and loss of heat is directly proportional to pressure.

In general the heat losses or reduced as the pressure is decreased and in conclusion the temperature of the filament increases. As the pressure falls below 102 torr, no collision with the wall decrease thus making change in temperature of the filament is negligible thus the gage becomes insensitive at low pressure. [3]

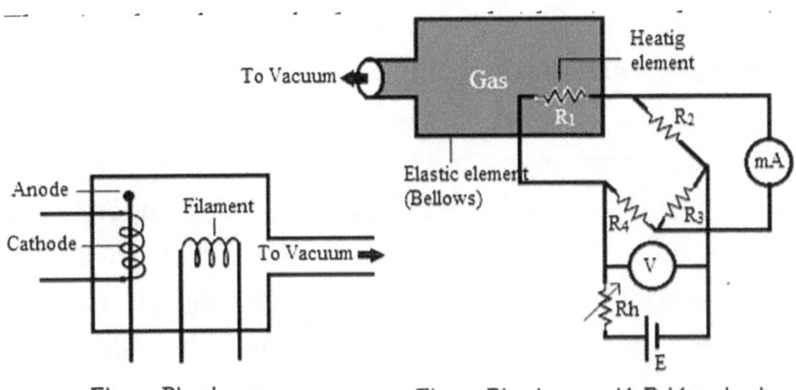

Figure: Pirani gage   Figure: Pirani gage with Bridge circuit

The filament is one arm i.e. 'R_1' is a variable resistor. R_2 and R_3 are equal resistors. The filament is one arm along with the cylinder is attached to vacuum of which pressure is measured. At very low pressure i.e. 10-3 micron the input voltage is set at some value say V_o at R_1. To obtain the balancing condition adjusts R_1. As the pressure decreases heat conducted away from the filament decreases therefore temperature and hence the resistance of the filament increases. Bridge voltage is again adjusted to have the original balancing condition. The measurement of the pressure is the measurement of rebalance voltage of the bridge i.e. $P = \text{constant } (V_c^2 - V_o^2)$.

7.3. Pressure calibration (Dead weight tester):

A dead weight tester is commonly used for static calibration of pressure measuring devices. The pressure in the tester is build till the weights are seen to be float, when the fluid gage pressure equals the dead weight divided by the piston area. The following figure shows tentative idea about the dead weight tester.

It consists of two accurately machined cylinders inserted into two closed and known cross sectional areas coupled together to a cylinder. One of the cylinders is fitted with a top platform where accurately known weights in the form of disc can be loaded. The transducer under test is connected to the other cylinder. The fluid pressure is then gradually applied until the force is large enough to just lift the precision piston weight combination. When the piston is floating freely, the piston gauge with arrange weight is in equilibrium with the pressure developed in the cylinder. [4, 5]

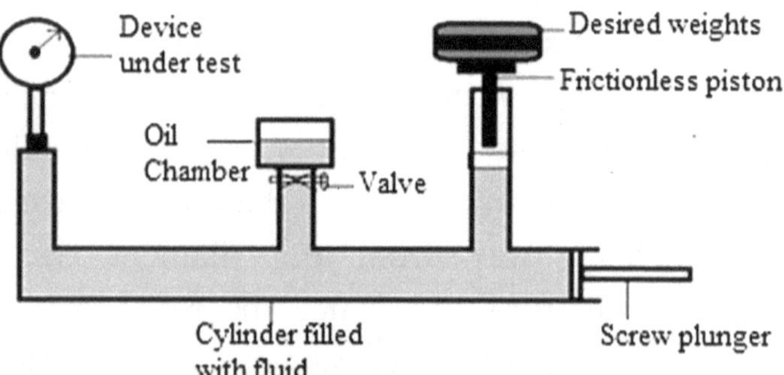

Figure : Construction of Dead Weight Tester

The relationship can be expressed as

$$F = P\,A$$

Where 'F' is the equivalent force of the piston weight combination (total mass x acceleration due to gravity) corrected for local gravity and floating air. 'P'' is pressure and 'A' is the equivalent area of the piston cylinder combination. It is necessary that this cylinder and piston head are perfectly vertical. To reduce this friction created by the fluid field, the piston is rotated or vibrated by changing the weights appropriately. The sensor can be calibrated to a high order of accuracy.

7.4. High pressure measurement:

When pressure above 103 atmospheres is to be measure, special techniques are used. One such a technique is based on change in electrical resistance. The filament is used in this technique is especially of magnin (alloy of copper, Ni, Mn). The construction of a device which is used to measure the high pressure is as shown in the following figure.

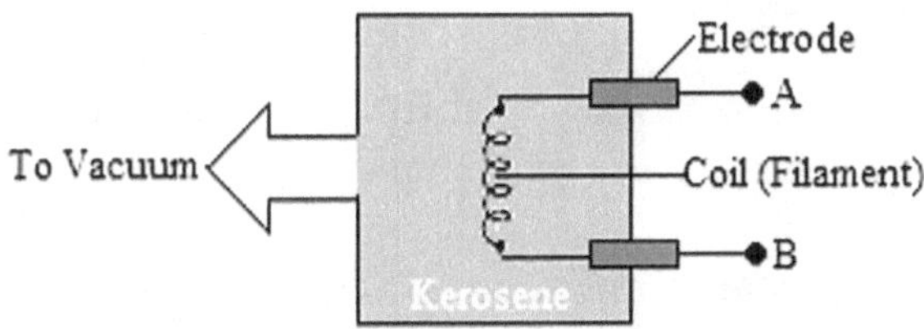

Figure: Experimental setup to measure high Pressure

The device consists usually a coil, which is enclosed in a flexible bellows, filled with kerosene. The kerosene is used to transmit the pressure which is to be measure. Due to change in pressure, temperature gets change; conversely there is change in the resistance of the wire. The ends of the wires say A and B are the one of the arm of the bridge. Hence using the null method of the bridge balance, the pressure is to be calculated. The value of the resistance R can be calculated using the formula,

$$R = \frac{4\rho L}{\pi d^2}$$

Where, L- length of the filament, D the diameter of the filament and ρ be the resistivity constant. The filament of gold is more preferred than any other material, as it is more sensitive to tempearture changes.

References

1. http://www.hds.bme.hu/mota/eng/ime/IME4_Pressure_and_Flow_Rate.pdf

2. http://encyclopedia2.thefreedictionary.com/McLeod+gauge

3. Pressure sensors, http://www.ni.com/white-paper/14847/en/

4. https://grabcad.com/requests/dead-weight-tester.

5. http://instrumentationandcontrollers.blogspot.com/2010/10/dead-weight-tester.

8. Measurement of flow

8.1. Introduction:

The flow measurements include the measurement of flow rate of solids, liquids and gases. Basically there are ways of flow measurement volumetric basis and the other on the basis of weight. Solid materials are measured in terms of either weight per unit time or mass per unit time. Very rarely solid quantity is measured in terms of volume. Liquids are measured either in volume rate or in weight rate. Gases are normally measured in volume rate.

There are two types Fluids incompressible and compressible. Fluids in liquid phase are incompressible whereas fluids in gaseous phase are compressible. Liquid occupies the same volume at different pressures where as gases occupy different volumes at different pressures. Taking into account this fact the calibration of flow meters are calibrated. The measurements taken at actual conditions should be converted either to Standard temperature (0°C) and pressure (760 mm Hg).

There are two types of fluid flows.

Streamline flow and turbulent flow. When the liquid is in motion, the velocity of liquid at each and every point remains constant, the flow is said to be Stream line flow. When the velocity does not remains same when the fluid is moving the flow is said to be turbulent flow.

Flow meter is a device that measures the rate of flow or quantity of a moving fluid in an open or closed channel. Flow measuring devices are classified into four groups.

1. Mechanical type flow meters: Fixed restriction variable head type flow meters using different sensors like Venturi tube, Orifice plate, flow nozzle, Pitot tube, quantity meters like positive displacement meters, mass flow meters etc. These types of devices are under the head of mechanical type flow meters.

2. Inferential type flow meters: Variable area flow meters (Rotameters), turbine flow meter, target flow meters etc.

3. Electrical type flow meters: Ultrasonic flow meter, Electromagnetic flow meter, Laser Doppler Anemometers etc.

4. Other flow meters: Flow meters for Solids flow measurement, Cross-correlation flow meter, flow switches etc.[1]

8.2. Bernoulli's principle:

Bernoulli's principle is related with the movement of a fluid through a pressure difference. Suppose a fluid is moving in a horizontal direction and come across a pressure difference, this pressure difference will result in a net force, which will causes an acceleration of the fluid by the Newton's second law of motion.

We know the fundamental relation,

Work done = Change in Kinetic energy,

Therefore, (Change in Pressure) x Area x distance = Change in Kinetic energy,

It means, Change Pressure + Change in (Kinetic energy/Volume) = 0

So that, Pressure+ Kinetic energy/Volume = constant --------- (A)

Equation (A) is known as Bernoulli's equation. Bernoulli's principle states that a rise or fall in pressure in a flowing fluid must always be accompanied by a decrease or increase in the speed, and conversely, if an increase or decrease in the speed of the fluid results in a decrease or increase in the pressure. For example, a shower curtain gets sucked inwards when the water is first turned on. The increased water or air velocity inside the curtain relative to the air on the other side causes a pressure drop. The pressure difference between the outside and inside causes a net force on the shower curtain which sucks it inward.

8.2.1. Bernoulli's theorem:

The theorem states that in a fluid stream the sum of pressure head, velocity head and gravitational or elevation head at a point is equal to their sum at any other point move in the direction of flow from the first point to the other point plus the loss due to friction between the two points.

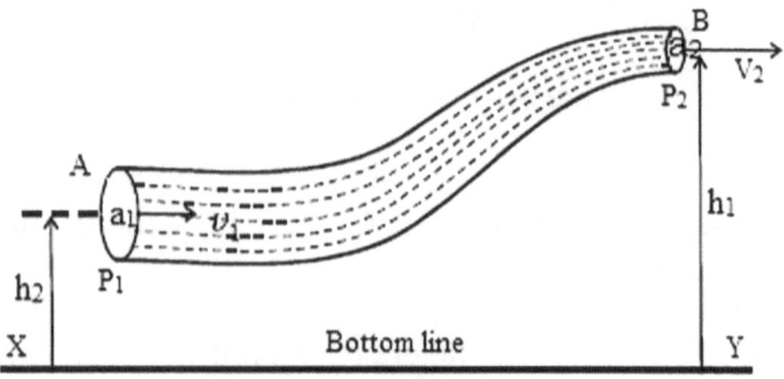

Figure : Bernoullis Theorem

Consider a flow tube of varying cross sectional area and having a difference in levels as shown in above figure. An incompressible fluid of density 'ρ' is assumed to be steadily flowing through the pipe with its axis inclined above the horizontal line XY. If we assume that P_1, V_1, be the pressure, velocity of the fluid flow at the entering end. P_2, V_2, be the pressure and velocity of the fluid flow at the leaving end. h_1 and h_2 be the distance from the bottom line at the respective ends of the pipeline and 'g' be acceleration due to gravity and k be the constant.[2]

Making the use of the principle of law of conversation of energy, the work done on a mass of fluid minus the work done by it is equal to its change in potential energy and kinetic energy. Applying this principle the relationship for the fluid flow under equilibrium conditions can be expressed as,

$$\frac{P_1}{\rho} + \frac{V_1^2}{2g} + h_1 = \frac{P_2}{\rho} + \frac{V_2^2}{2g} + h_2 = \text{Constant K} \quad \text{------------ (1)}$$

If the levels of the pipeline are same, means $h_1 = h_2$ then equation (1) becomes,

$$\frac{P_1}{\rho} + \frac{V_1^2}{2g} = \frac{P_2}{\rho} + \frac{V_2^2}{2g} \qquad (2)$$

If the flow is continuous then the quantity of fluid, the fluid passing per second at the entering end must be equal to the fluid passing per second at the leaving end, called as the equation of continuity.

$$\text{i.e. } a_1 v_1 = a_2 v_2 \qquad (3)$$

$$V_1 = \frac{a_2 v_2}{a_1} = X v_2 \qquad (4)$$

$$V_2^2 - V_1^2 = (P_1 - P_2)\frac{2g}{\rho} \qquad (5)$$

Therefore equation 5 takes the form,

$$v_2^2 - X^2 v_2^2 = \frac{2g\,(P_1 - P_2)}{\rho}$$

$$v_2^2\,(1 - X^2) = \frac{2g\,(P_1 - P_2)}{\rho}$$

$$v_2^2 = \frac{2g\,(P_1 - P_2)}{\rho\,(1 - X^2)}$$

Therefore,

$$V_2 = \sqrt{\frac{2g(p_1 - p_2)}{\rho}} \times \frac{1}{(1 - X^2)}$$

As we know that $Q = av$, the rate of flow, it can be obtain by multiplying both sides to above equation by a_2, we can get,

$$Q = a_2 V_2 = a_2 \sqrt{\frac{2g(p_1-p_2)}{\rho}} \times \frac{1}{(1-X^2)}$$

Threfore,

$$Q = E a_2 \sqrt{\frac{2g(p_1-p_2)}{\rho}} \text{------------(6)}$$

Where, E is called as velocity approach factor and is equal to,

$$E = \sqrt{\frac{1}{(1-X^2)}}$$

The last equation (6) shows that, shows that the flow rate of fluid can be conventionally commuted by an accurate measurement of the differential pressure developed and by knowing the other constants.

In case, when the pipeline is not parallel to the bottom line ($h_1 \neq h_2$) then the height difference should take into account, hence the equation (6) can be written as,

$$Q = E a_2 \sqrt{\frac{2g(p_1-p_2) + (h_1-h_2)\rho}{\rho}}$$

In this equation $h_1 - h_2$ represents the elevation head and the term, $(P_1-P_2) + (h_1-h_2)\,\rho$ represents the pressure difference (Pd) and hence the above equation can also be written as,

$$Q = Ea_2 \sqrt{\frac{2g\,Pd}{\rho}} \quad \text{--------(7)}$$

8.3. β Ratio:

The most variable head meters depend on a restriction in the flow path to produce a change in velocity. For the circular pipe, the Beta ratio is the ratio between the diameter of the restriction and the inside diameter of the pipe.

$$\beta = d/D$$

Where d = diameter of the restriction D = inside diameter of the pipe.

8.4. Reynolds Number:

In practice, flow velocity at any cross section approaches zero in the boundary layer adjacent to the pipe wall and varies across the diameter. This flow velocity has an important effect on the relationship between flow velocity and pressure difference developed in the head meters. To describe this phenomenon, Sir Osborne Reynolds proposed single, dimensionless ratio known as Reynolds number, as a criterion. This number Re, is expressed as

$$Re = \rho\,\mu\,VD,$$

Where V = velocity, D = Diameter of the pipeline, ρ = density and μ = absolute viscosity.

Reynolds number expresses the ratio of inertial forces to viscous forces.

When Reynolds number is high, the inertial forces predominate and viscous effects become negligible. At a very low Reynolds number, viscous forces predominate and inertial forces have little effect.

8.5. Discharge Coefficient (Cd):

The Discharge coefficient, 'Cd' is the ratio between actual volumetric flow rate and ideal volumetric flow rate.

$$Cd = q_{actual} / q_{ideal}$$

Where q_{actual} = Actual volumetric flow rate and q_{ideal} = Ideal volumetric flow rate. [3]

8.6. U- Tube manometer:

The manometers are the devices in which columns of a suitable liquid are used to measure the difference in pressure between the two points. Manometer is used to measure the large gage pressures. A common type of U-tube manometer is as shown in the following figure.

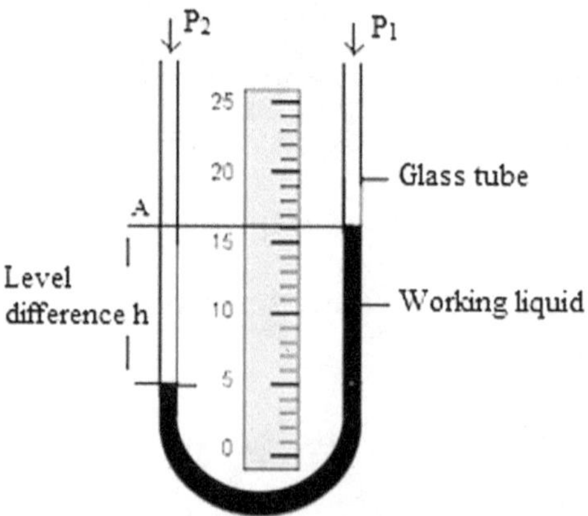

Figure: U-tube manometer

One of the ends of the manometer is connected to pipe or a container having fluid (x) whose pressure is to be measured while the other end is open to the atmosphere. The power part of the u-tube contains a liquid immiscible with the fluid(x) and is of greater density than that of the fluid x. This fluid is called as manometric fluid. The pressure between the two points A and B in the horizontal plane within the continuous expansion of the same fluid must be equal. Equating the pressures at B and C, in terms of the heights of the fluids above those points, with the fundamental equation of hydrostatics, we can get, P = (height difference between the points A and B) x ρg = hgρ. [4]

8.7. Venturimeter/Venturi tube:

The Venturi meter/tube measures the rate of flow of liquid through pipe based on Bernoulli's theorem. The Venturi meter was devised by Hershel an American engineer in 1886 and an Italian engineer venture was developed this device.

The principle of the device is that, "when liquid flows through a tube of varying cross sectional areas the velocity and pressure vary along the tube. We know that the relation between pressure and velocity is inversely proportional. The following figure is the tentative idea of venture meter.

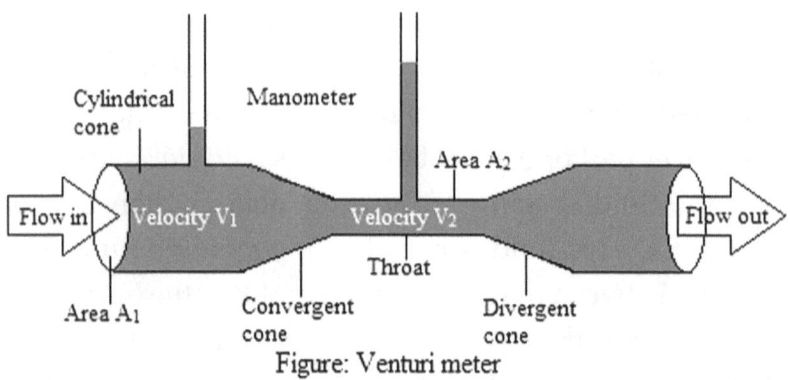

Figure: Venturi meter

As shown in above figure, the tube of venturi meter having area 'A$_1$' at its entering ends while 'A$_2$' be the area where the tube converges. This total area called as 'throat' or 'vena- contract'. In the throat area, the velocity of the liquid increases conversely the pressure gets reduced. The velocity of the liquid may regain at the leaving end of the tube, but does not reach to its initial value. It means that there is a permanent loss in pressure. This loss depends on the dimension of the devices and the type of restriction. The ratio of the diameter at the constriction to the diameter of the pipe is called as the 'diameter ratio'. If this ratio is small the opening is narrow and the pressure loss become considerable but the efficiency of the measurement is low. If this ratio is too large, the opening is wide; the reduction in pressure is too small for accurate measurements. [5]

Let P_1, V_1 and P_2, V_2 be the pressure and velocity at the entering end and at the throat respectively. ρ

From Bernoulli theorem,

$$\frac{P_1}{\rho} + \frac{V_1^2}{2} = \frac{P_2}{\rho} + \frac{V_2^2}{2}$$

Let us assume that, the device is placed horizontal.

From equation of the continuity, i.e. the rate of discharge of fluid is,

$$Q = A_1 V_1 = A_2 V_2$$

i.e. $\quad V_1 = \dfrac{A_2}{A_1} V_2 = \dfrac{Q}{A_1}\quad$ similarly $\quad V_2 = \dfrac{Q}{A_2}$

Therefore, $\quad \dfrac{P_1}{\rho} - \dfrac{P_2}{\rho} = \dfrac{1}{2}(V_2^2 - V_1^2)$

i.e. $\quad \dfrac{P_1}{\rho} - \dfrac{P_2}{\rho} = \dfrac{1}{2}\left[\dfrac{Q^2}{A_2^2} - \dfrac{Q^2}{A_1^2}\right]$

i.e. $\quad \dfrac{P_1 - P_2}{\rho} = \dfrac{Q^2}{2}\left[\dfrac{A_1^2 - A_2^2}{A_1^2 . A_2^2}\right]$

i.e. $\quad Q^2 = \dfrac{2A_1^2 A_2^2 (P_1 - P_2)}{\rho (A_1^2 - A_2^2)}$

Therefore, $\quad Q = A_1 A_2 \sqrt{\dfrac{2h\rho g}{\rho (A_1^2 - A_2^2)}}$

Therefore, $\quad Q = A_1 A_2 \sqrt{\dfrac{2gh}{A_1^2 - A_2^2}}$

Hence the above equation of rate of flow of fluid clears that, the rate of flow of fluid depends upon the area of cross section of the venturi tube.

8.8. Pitot tube:

A Pitot static system is a pressure sensitive instruments that is most often used to determine airspeed of an aircraft's, altitude and altitude trend. A Pitot-static system consists of a Pitot tube, a static port, and the Pitot-static instruments. This equipment is used to measure the forces acting on a vehicle as a function of the temperature, density, pressure and viscosity of the fluid in which it is operating. Commonly used variable head velocity measuring device is the pitot static tube usually called simply Pitot tube. It is perhaps better known as air speed indicator used in aircraft. The following figure shows a schematic diagram of the Pitot tube. It consist of two concentrically arranged tube bent at right angles, the inner tube (stagnant tube) is open ended and faces the oncoming stream of fluid impinges. This open end is brought to rest and its kinetic energy is converted to the pressure head, commonly known as velocity head.

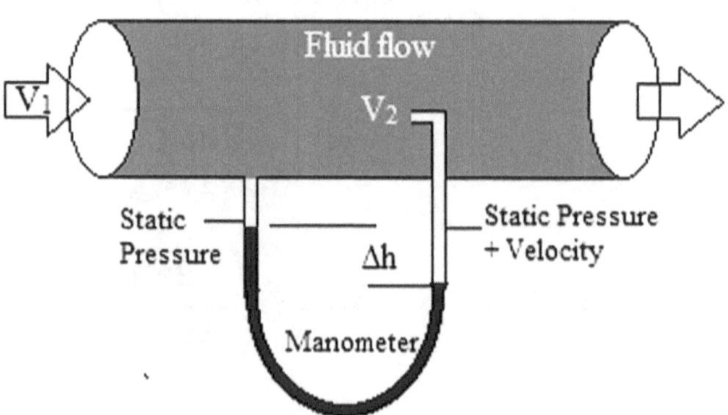

Figure: Tentative sketch of Pitot tube

According to Bernoulli's theorem, the sum of pressure head, velocity head and elevation head remains constant. P

$$\frac{P_1}{\rho}+\frac{V_1^2}{2g}+h_1=\frac{P_2}{\rho}+\frac{V_2^2}{\rho}+h_2=\text{Constant K} \quad\text{———(1)}$$

$$\frac{P_1}{\rho}+\frac{V_1^2}{2}=\frac{P_2}{\rho}+\frac{V_2^2}{2} \qquad \text{where, } h_1 = h_2$$

Here the velocity $V_2 = 0$

$$\frac{P_1}{\rho}+\frac{V_1^2}{2}=\frac{P_2}{\rho}$$

$$\frac{P_1-P_2}{\rho}=-\frac{V_1^2}{2}$$

$$\frac{P_2-P_1}{\rho}=\frac{V_1^2}{2}$$

$$\text{Therefore,} \quad V_1=\sqrt{\frac{2(P_1-P_2)}{\rho}}$$

$$\text{Therefore,} \quad V_1=\sqrt{\frac{2h.\rho.g}{\rho}}$$

$$\text{Hence, } V_1=\sqrt{2gh}$$

$$Q = a_1v_1 = a_1\sqrt{2gh}$$

The rate of flow of fluid i.e. the volume of fluid flowing per second across any section.

8.9. Rotameter:

In the variable area flow meter, the differential pressure remains constant across the meter, a Rotameter is under this class of flow meter. The first variable area meter with rotating float was invented by Karl Kueppers in 1908. It was first manufactured by Rotawerke Company and so it is recognized as a Rotameter. The following figure depicts the superficial idea about the Rotameter. [6]

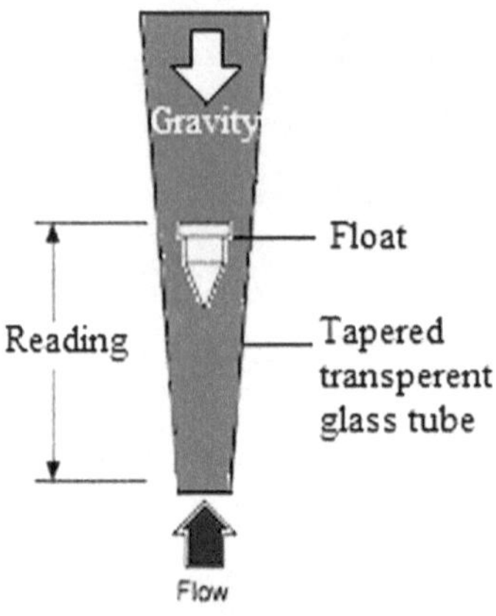

Figure: Rotameter

A Rotameter consists of a tapered glass/metal tube, with a 'float'. The float made either of anodized aluminum or a ceramic. Floats are made in many different shapes may be spheres, ellipsoids or any other required shapes. To rotate the float axially when the fluid passes it may be diagonally grooved and partially colored. The "float" should have higher density than fluid otherwise it will on the top of the fluid.

The float will rise to a point in the tube where the dragged force i.e. f drag (upward direction) and the buoyant force i.e. f buoyant (upward direction) is balanced by the weight of float (downward). The position of the float in the tube is taken as an indication of the flow rate i.e.

$$f_{drag} + f_{buoyant} = f_{weight\ of\ the\ bob}$$

Readings are usually taken at the top of the widest part of the float and depends on the shape of the float and the manufacturers. A higher volumetric flow rate through a given area increases flow speed and drag force, so the float will be pushed upwards. However the Rotameter has the shape of conical tapered so that the area around the float through which the medium flows increases so that, the flow speed and drag force decrease until there is mechanical equilibrium with the float's weight.

References

1. www.idc.online.com/technical_references/pdfs/instrumentation/Industrial_Instru.

2. www.physics365.com/blog/?page_id=2678

3. Ref: industrial instrumentation C-8\N-IND\BOOK

4. www.efunda.com/formulae/fluids/manometer.

5. http://pixshark.com/venturi-meter.htm

6. www.eq.uc.pt/~lferreira/BIBL_SEM/global/rotametro/imagens

9. Acoustic measurement

9.1. Introduction:

Sound waves are a particular form of waves known as elastic waves. Elastic waves can occur in media having the properties of mass i.e. inertia and elasticity. Sound wares or acoustic pulses that consist of succession of rapid variation in air pressure usually of small magnitudes. Sound waves are transmitted through the fluid and produce the sensation of hearing mechanism. Acoustical measurement finds the wide applications in our day to day life, for example noise control studies i.e. the development of less noisy machinery and equipments.

9.2. Characteristics of sound:

- Sound intensely in W/m^2 or its pressure in microbar. ($1\mu bar = 1dyne/cm^2$).

- Its frequency in cycle/sec or hertz (Hz).

- Nature of noise which may be either continuous or impulsive.

- It loudness or loudness level.

- Its noise reading also called as annoyance rating based on SPL and frequency.

Decibel:

The quantity decibel represents a relative measurement or ratio. Each quantity measured in decibel i.e. db is expressed as a ratio relative to a reference power, pressure intensity or whatever quantity are considered. Decibel comes from 'Bel' and was evolved in 1922 to describe the attenuation in signals in telephone cables by graham Bel. The Bel ratio was found to be very large and hence decibel was introduced. [1]

The Bel ratio was, $\mathrm{Log}_{10} R = 1$ i.e. $R = 10^1 = 10$.

While, decibel ratio is $\log_{10} r = 0.1 = 10^{0.1} = 1.26$

9.3. Sound pressure level (SPL):

The audible range of human being hearing mechanism usually measured at 1kHz. It is extending from 0.0002 μbar at threshold of hearing of to 1 mbar at the threshold of pain. This represents an increased of 5×10^6, because of this very large range, the magnitude of sound pressure is expressed in logarithmic scales, in terms of decibel.

Sound pressure level i.e. SPL is defined as follows,

$$SPL = 10 \log \frac{P^2}{P_{ref}^2}$$

$$\text{i.e.} \quad SPL = 20 \log \frac{P}{P_{ref}} \quad \text{in dB}$$

Where P is r.m.s value of sound pressure and Pref is the r.m.s value of reference pressure. The reference pressure has been chosen as the smallest possible sound level at 1 KHz, that young adult can just hear and is taken as,

0.0002 bar = 0.0002 dynes/cm² = 0.00002 N/m².

Hence Sound Pressure Level is measured as follows,

$$\text{i.e.} \quad SPL = 20 \log \frac{P}{0.0002}$$

Some typical sound SPL values are given below,

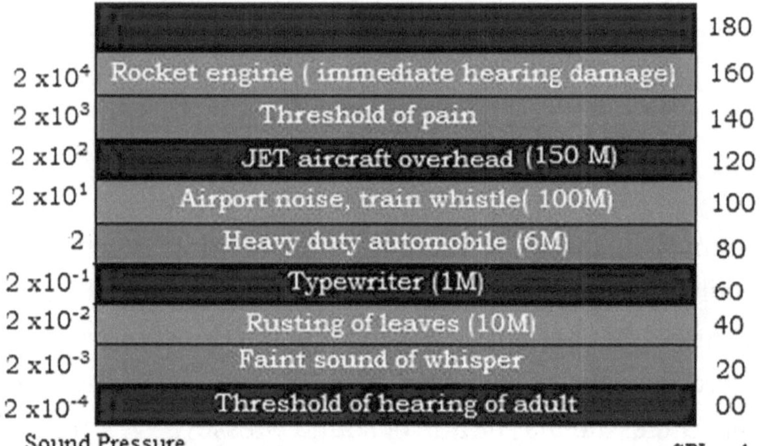

Figure : Typical SPL values of some sounds

9.4. Sound power levels (PWL):

Sound power means the total energy radiated by a sound source per unit time. It is often abbreviated as PWL. The sound power level (PWL) defined as the ratio of actual power of the sound to the reference power of the sound.

$$\text{i.e.} \quad PWL = 10 \log \frac{W}{W_{ref}} \quad \text{in dB}$$

Where 'W' is the acoustics power of the source, 'W_{ref}' is reference acoustics power. The reference power 'W_{ref}' is taken as 10^{-12} watt. The power can be as low as 10^{-9} watt at a faint whisper or 10-5 watt at a normal conversational speech. The sound power level is as large as 10mw for Saturn rocket or 50kw for a jet air lines.

Some typical examples of sound power level are given as below.

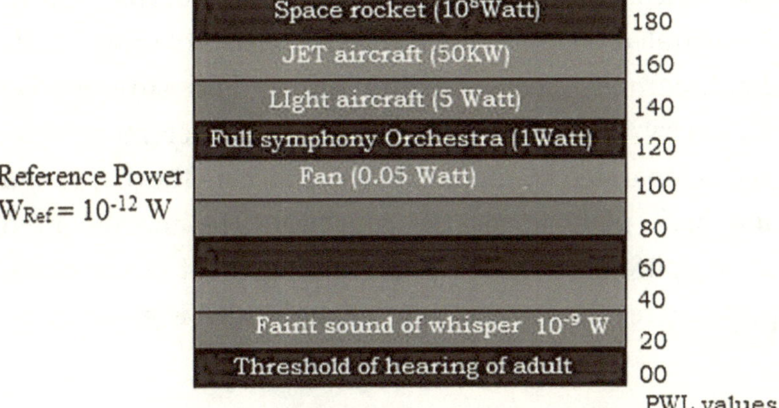

Figure : Typical PWL values of some sounds   (in dB)

9.5. Microphones:

Microphones are transducers that coverts sound pressure variation into the analog electrical signal. The sensitivity, frequency response, dynamic range and linearity are the factor one should take into account whenever there is selection of Microphone.

Microphones generally make use of a thin diaphragm to convert pressure into motion. This motion is then converted into suitable electrical output by employing secondary transducer. The transducer used for this purpose may be either of the following type.

1) Condenser type

2) Electro dynamic type

3) Carbon granule's type

9.5.1. Condenser type microphone:

The typical construction of condenser type of microphone is illustrated on following figure. It consists of thin metallic diaphragm in close proximity to a rigid support, say stationary back plate. We know condenser means two plates separated by dielectric material, here the diaphragm and back plate forms the capacitor. The movement of the diaphragm caused by the impingement of the sound pressure result in an output voltage, which is given by

$$E \sim Qd$$

Where 'Q' is the charge provided by the polarizing voltage and d be the distance between the plate and 'E' is the output voltage of the capacitor.

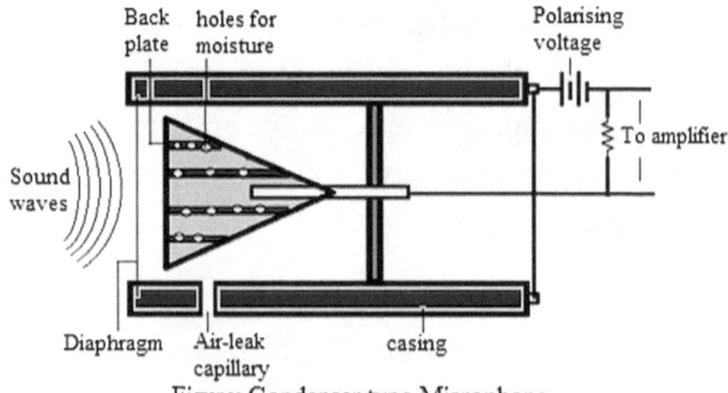

Figure: Condenser type Microphone

An air leak capillary is used to equalization of pressures on both the sides of the diaphragm to prevent the microphone from the bursting. The back plate is provided with damping holes; the motion of the diaphragm causes air flow through the holes which results in energy dissipation because of the fluid friction. The damping effect is make use to control of the resonant peaks of the diaphragm response. [2]

9.5.2. Electrodynamics type microphone:

These microphones are based on the principle of generation of EMF, when a moving conductor is placed in a magnetic field. The following figure depicts a typical construction of electrodynamics microphone.

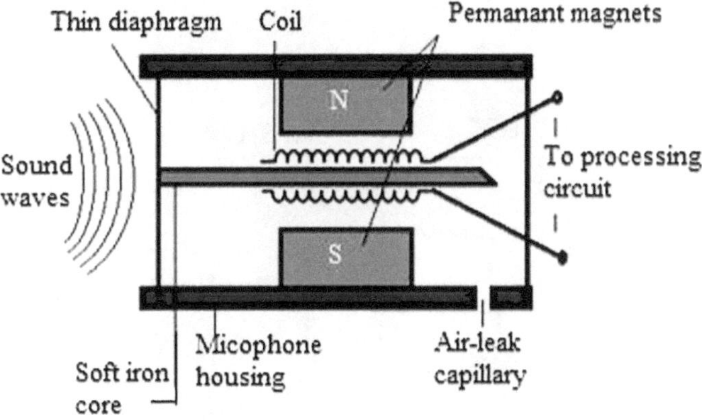

Figure: Electrodynamic type microphone

The sensing diaphragm is attached to a coil placed within the poles of permanent magnets. The movement of the diaphragm due to acoustics/sound pressure generates the analogous included voltage in the coil. The obvious advantage of such microphones have are of being self generating devices but due to the high inertia of the moving coil their frequency response remains very poor. [3]

9.5.3. Carbon granules type microphone:

The carbon granules microphone means the microphone works on the carbon granules. This type of microphone consists of capsules which are filled with the granules of carbon. Due to the sound pressure, which is sensed by diaphragm, the resistance of carbon granules gets changed. The following figure clears the construction of carbon granules type microphone. These types of microphones are generally used in telephone transmission circuit as they are relatively inexpensive and are also ragged in construction.

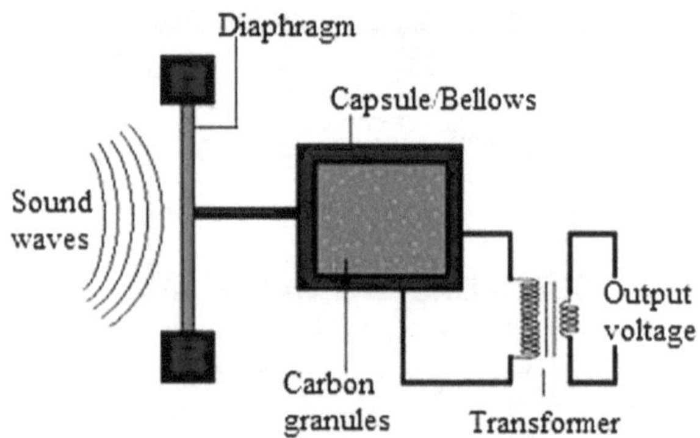

Figure: Carbon granules type Microphone

There frequency response and the linearity characteristic are very poor hence they are not used for accurate measurement of sound. [4]

9.6. Loudness:

One of the characteristic of a sound is the Loudness. It is primarily a psychological correlate of physical strength. Loudness is a subjective measure. The physical response of the people to sound pressure level is different for different frequency. The SPL necessary at each frequency to produce the same loudness response to a listener is different. A higher SPL is required at low frequency than that at higher frequency to produce the same loudness sensation. However, loudness perception is a much more complex process. Loudness is also affected by parameters other than sound pressure, including frequency, bandwidth and duration. For example if the magnitude of SPL at 1 KHz in 40 dB it means that its loudness level at 1 KHz frequency is 40 Phons.

9.7. Sound Level meter:

SPL are measured by SLM which correct acoustics pressure into voltage. The block diagram of device is as shown in figure.

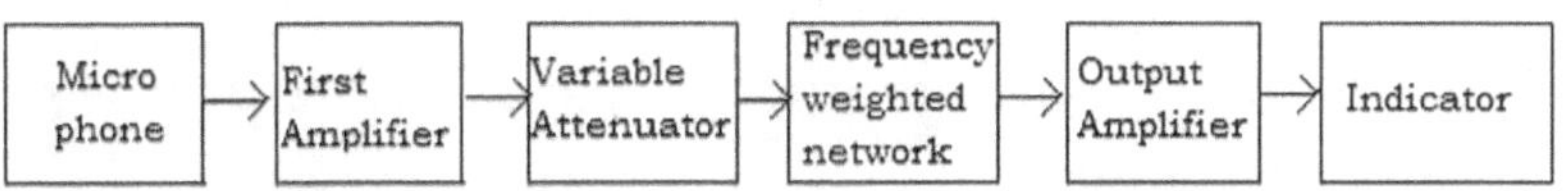

Figure: Block digram of sound level meter

It consists of a high quality microphone to intercept the noise to be measure. The output of the microphone is given to the first amplifier or preamplifier. The output of the preamplifier is fed to the variable attenuator providing the various ranges. The signal then passes through the frequency weighted network to separate output amplifiers for output, the output amplifier, and to a suitable indicating instrument such as a vacuum-tube voltmeter. There must be provisions for calibrating the circuit, either by using a standard tone, or by other means. The separate amplifiers are used so that meter reading   independent of loading on the output and so that the signal at the output does not distorted by the nonlinear meter element. The frequency-weighting network weights the various frequency components of a complex noise wave in accordance with the characteristics of the ear. The ear does not have the same characteristics at different loudness levels. Thus, for sounds of a level of 50 db, the ear has the characteristics given by the 50-db loudness-level contour, For a 60-db sound, the characteristics are as given by curve 60, and for very intense sounds of about 100 db, the characteristics of the ear are essentially flat. [5]

References

1. https://en.wikipedia.org/wiki/Sound_pressure.

2. www.mediacollege.com/audio/microphones/condenser.html

3. Sound transducer, www.electronics-tutorials.ws/io/io_8.html

4. www.schoolphysics.co.uk/age11-14/Electricity   and magnetism/Electromagnetism/text/Carbon microphone

5. www.vias.org/albert_ecomm/aec02_acoustic_fundamentals_020.html

10. Measurement of magnetic field

10.1. Introduction:

Top of Form

Magnetism is a force of attraction or repulsion that acts at a distance. It is due to a magnetic field, which is caused by moving electrically charged particles or is inherent in magnetic objects such as a magnet. A magnet is an object that exhibits a strong magnetic field and will attract materials like iron to it. Magnetism has many uses in modern life. A magnetic field consists of unreal lines of flux coming from moving electrically charged particles. If a larger object exhibits a sufficiently great magnetic field, it is called a magnet. The magnetic field of an object can produce a magnetic force on other objects with magnetic fields. That force is called as magnetism. When a magnetic field is applied to a moving electric charge, such as electrical current in a wire, the force on the charge is called as Lorentz force. The magnetic and electric fields are similar and so they are inter-related. In electric field the positive (+) and negative (−) electrical charges attract each other while North 'N' and south 'S' poles of a magnet attract each other. The magnetic field is a dipole field but the electrical charges are called monopoles, because they can exist without the opposite charge.

There are permanent magnets, temporary magnets and electromagnets. A permanent magnet keeps its magnetic properties for a long time. Magnetite is a permanent magnet but it is relatively weak. Most of the permanent magnets in the laboratory use are manufactured and of a combination or alloy of iron, nickel and cobalt. A temporary magnet loses its magnetism in a short while.

By wrapping a wire around an iron core and passing an electrical current through the wire, an electromagnet forms. If the core is soft iron, the magnetism will diminish as soon as the current is turned off. This feature makes electromagnets good for picking up and dropping objects.

A compass is simply a thin magnet or magnetized iron needle balanced on a pivot. It can be used to detect small magnetic fields. The needle will rotate to point toward the opposite pole of a magnet. It can be very sensitive to small magnetic fields. We know, Earth is a giant magnet.

Gauss meters are used to measure the strength of a magnetic field. A Hall strip is use called as a Hall Effect device, which gives off a tiny electrical current when exposed to a magnetic field. There are three main factors that determine the magnetic property of a material.

- The configuration of the electrons in the material atoms.
- The ability of the atoms or molecules in the material to align magnetically.
- The alignment of domains in a material.

Electrons can behave as tiny magnets, the atom becomes like a magnet, in fact when electrons move they create a magnetic field. A magnetic field is also created when electrons rotate around a nucleus and when they spin while in orbit. This spinning creates a magnetic field. If the metals typically respond well to a magnetic field–such as iron and nickel–then their alloy has even a stronger reaction to magnetism.

The final factors in a material being magnetic concern the orientation of its domains in a solid. A group of atoms in a metal may become aligned, but the various groups may be misaligned. These groups are called domains. [1, 2]

10.2. Classifications of Magnetic Materials:

Materials respond differently to the force of a magnetic field. There are three main types of magnetic materials. A magnet will strongly attract ferromagnetic materials, weakly attract paramagnetic materials and weakly repel diamagnetic materials.

10.2.1. Ferromagnetic materials:

Ferromagnetic materials are strongly attracted by a magnetic force. In the class of ferromagnetic, the elements iron (Fe), cobalt (Co), nickel (Ni), and gadolinium (Gd) are the materials. These metals are strongly attracted because of their individual atoms have a slightly higher degree of magnetism due to their configuration of electrons, their atoms readily line up in the same magnetic direction and the magnetic domains or groups of atoms line up more readily. Iron is the most common element which is attracted to a magnet. Steel is also a ferromagnetic material. Steel retains magnetism longer than iron because of its hardness. There are number of materials like alloys of iron, nickel, cobalt, gadolinium and certain ceramic materials can become "permanent" magnets, such that they retain their magnetism for a long time.

If strong magnetic ferromagnetic materials like nickel or steel are heated at a very high temperature then they lose all their magnetic properties. The atoms become too excited by the heat to remain pointing in one direction for long time. The temperature at which a metal loses its total magnetism called as the 'Curie temperature' and this Curie temperature is different for every metal. The Curie temperature for nickel is approximately about 350°C.

10.2.2. Paramagnetic materials:

The materials which are weakly attracted to magnets are the paramagnetic materials. Aluminum and copper metals are the well known examples of this class. These materials can become very weak magnets, but their attractive force can only be measured with sensitive instruments. Temperature can affect the magnetic properties of a material. At very low temperature the paramagnetic materials like aluminum, uranium and platinum can become more magnetic. The force of a ferromagnetic magnet is very large as compared to magnet made with a paramagnetic material. The attractive force of paramagnetic materials is very small, so these are typically considered as nonmagnetic.

10.2.3. Diamagnetic materials:

When the materials are exposed to a strong magnetic field, they induce a weak magnetic field in the opposite direction. Certain materials are diamagnetic; it means that they weakly repel a strong magnet. Bismuth and carbon graphite are the strongest diamagnetic materials. Water, diamonds, wood and living tissue etc are the materials in this class.

When an electric current passes through a wire, i.e. an electrical charge is moving, a circular magnetic field is generated. The direction of the magnetic field can be determined by the right-hand rule. The Right hand rule states that "When an electric charge moves through a magnetic field, there is a force on the charge, perpendicular to the direction of the charge and perpendicular to the direction of the magnetic field. This force is called as the Lorentz Force".

Magnetic materials are further classified as soft or hard materials according to the ability of magnetization. In AC generators and transformers are the examples of soft materials in which change in the magnetization during operation is desirable. Hard materials are used to supply a fixed field either to act alone, as in a magnetic separator, or to interact with others, as in loudspeakers and instruments. The magnetic hysteresis curve is the characterization technique for both the materials. [3]

10.2.4. Soft magnetic Materials:

Soft magnetic material means they do not retain their magnetism when removed from a magnetic field, these are also called as electromagnets. These materials are characterized by their low loss and high permeability. There are a variety of alloys used with various combinations of magnetic properties, mechanical properties, and cost. Some materials which are available commercially are iron and low-carbon steels, iron-silicon alloys, iron-aluminum-silicon alloys, nickel-iron alloys, iron-cobalt alloys, ferrites, and amorphous alloys.

10.2.5. Hard magnetic Materials:

Hard magnetic materials are Permanent magnets; they retain their magnetism though removed from a magnetic field. Cobalt is the major element used for obtaining magnetic properties in hard magnetic alloys. The hard magnetic materials are used in meters, loudspeakers, motors,, and in other number of devices. The Alnicos and the cobalt-samarium, iron-neodymium, iron-chromium-cobalt, and elongated single-domain (ESD) are some materials of this class. [4, 5]

10.3. Production of magnetic field:

There are different methods to produce the magnetic fields in the materials. The intense magnetic field of the order 105 oersted has been produced by Kapitza. The Kapitza setup for the production of magnetic field consists a ring magnet having a cone of uniform cross section 'S', the length 'L' permeability 'μ' and having N- no of windings carrying a current I Amperes. Then magnetic field 'H' is given by the following formula.

$$H = \frac{4\pi NI}{10[(L/\mu S) + d]}$$

Where,'d' be gap between the pole pieces. By reducing the gap between the pole pieces i.e. interspaces 'd' and by increasing the permeability and the cross section 'S', 'H' can increased. H can also be increased by increasing the amperes turns ratio.

i.e. $H \alpha n I$

10.3.1. Weiss and cotton's powerful electromagnets:

The powerful electromagnets have been designed by Weiss and cotton's. This electromagnet consists of tubular winding carry large current through which water flows. The conical pole pieces which are made of ferrocobalt of high permeability. The adjustment of height and orientation of the whole magnet is control by mechanical devices. The Weiss magnet had 105 Ampere turns in the excitation coils and gave a field of 5 x 104 Oersted between the poles. When the diameter of the butt ends of the conical pole tips was 3.6 mm & the distance between the butt ends was 1.1mm the direct current voltage was about 90 V and the current about 113 amperes.

10.3.2. Kapitza's method for the production of magnetic field:

Kapitza's produced intense magnetic field of the order of the 2 x105 oerested by means of discharge of large number of accumulator in series which sent a very strong current though a coil for a very short interval of time. Momentary current of great intensity can also be produced by the discharge of high voltage condenser through a coil. Oil immersed paper condenser of 50μf withstand a changing pressure of 2000V DC can be used. They can be charged by suitable generator and then could be suddenly discharge through the solenoid windings of a coil. There should not any core inside the solenoid as the field outside for exceeds that due to magnetization of iron. The current is passed for a very short time about 1/100 sec. The winding immersed in oil which provides good insulation is a coolant and act as a buffer for mechanical force developed. By varying the parameters and skilful designing of the coil Kapitza improve, exceeds in generating a magnetic field of 3.2×10^5Oe over the volume of about 3 cubic centimeter without any damage to coil by above technique.

10.4. Measurement of magnetic field:

Magnetic field strength can be measured using number of techniques. Each technique has its own property that makes it more suitable for the particular applications. These applications can be range from simply sensing the presence or change in the field to the precise measurements of a magnetic fields scalar and vector properties. Magnetic field sensors can be divided into vector component and scalar magnitude types. The vector types can be further divided into sensors that are used to measure low fields i.e. less than 1 mT and high fields i.e. greater than 1 mT. Instruments that measure low fields are commonly called as magnetometers while the instruments which measure the high fields are known as gauss meters.

The induction coil and fluxgate magnetometers are the most widely used vector measuring instruments rugged, reliable and relatively lass expensive than the other low field vector measuring instruments. The Hall Effect device is the oldest and most common high field vector sensor used in gauss meters. It is especially useful for measuring extremely high field i.e. greater than 1T.

The SI unit of magnetic induction is Tesla (T) and magnetic flux is measured in Weber's (Wb). A flux density of $1Wb/m^2$ is 1 Tesla. The SI unit of Tesla is equivalent to (Newton-second) / (Coulomb. meter). In CGS units, B is measured in gauss (G) and ($1T= 10^4G$). The H-field is measured in amperes per meters (A/m) in SI units and Oersteds in CGS units.

10.4.1. Measurement of magnetic field using search coil:

Search coil is a closed wound small coil of about 50,100 or 200 turns of fine wire and about a cross sectioned area of 1Sq cm. The following figure depicts the experimental set up for the measurement of magnetic field using search coil.

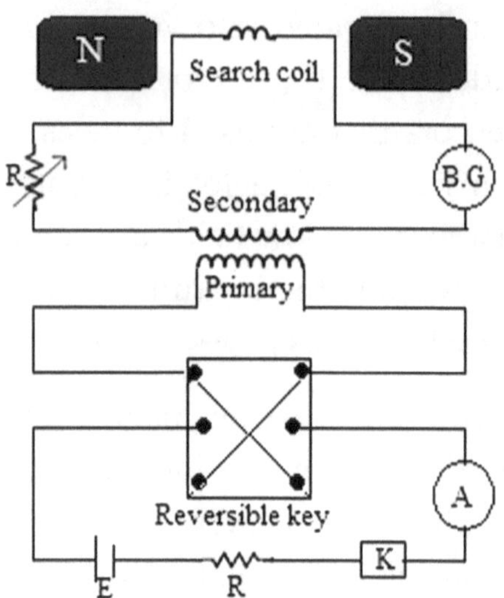

Figure : Experimental arrangement to
measure magnetic field using search coil

As shown in above figure the search coil is placed in the
gap between the two strong magnets with its plane normal
to the field. It is connected in series with a galvanometer
and secondary coil of solenoid. The primary winding
of solenoid is connected through a reversing key to the
battery, an ammeter and a variable resistor i.e. rheostat.
First of all the primary circuit of the solenoid is kept off and
the search coil inserted into the circuit, i.e. in the magnetic
induction 'B' which is to be measured.

If the search coil is placed with its plane perpendicular to a
magnetic induction then the magnetic flux linked with the
coil of turns 'N', each of area A, then $\Phi = BAN$.

If the coil placed not normal to a field then,

$$\Phi = BAN \cos\theta$$

Initially when the search coil is inserting with its plane perpendicular to the magnetic induction B and removed out quickly, the flux through the coil thus decreases rapidly from BAN to zero. At the same time the flux is decreasing and EMF of short duration is induced in the coil and hence a kick is imparted into the balancing galvanometer. If R be the resistance of the secondary circuit, then the amount of charge passing through the galvanometer is given as,

$$q_1 = \frac{BAN}{R}$$

If θ is the first throw of the Galvanometer due to this charge then,

$$q_1 = K\theta\,(1+\lambda/2) \text{----------- (A)}$$

Where K = Ballistic constant and λ = log decrement of Ballistic Galvanometer.

A known current 'i' flowing through the primary coil of the solenoid which can be reversed using a reversible and hence the corresponding throw of the ballistic galvanometer is observed and noted.

The magnetic field in the solenoid of N_1 turns per unit length due to current 'i' through it is,

$$B_s = \mu_0 n_1 i$$

Hence the total flux linked with the secondary coil of N_2 turns is,

$$\Phi = n_2 A_1 B_s$$

$$\Phi = n_2 A_1\, \mu_0 n_1 i$$

Where, A_1 be the area of each of secondary coil.

When the current in the primary is reversed then the magnetic flux linked with the secondary changes to, - $\mu_0 n_1 n_2 iA'$

Therefore net change in flux is $2\,\mu_0 n_1 n_2 iA'$

Thus, it is the net change produces kick in the galvanometer. If θ is the corresponding first throw then,

$$q' = \frac{2\,\mu_0 n_1 n_2 iA'}{R}$$

$$= K\theta(1+1/2\lambda) \text{----------(B)}$$

Using equation 1A and B, we can write the equation as,

$$\frac{BAN}{2\,\mu_0 n_1 n_2 iA'} = \frac{\theta}{\theta'}$$

$$\text{Or,} \quad B = \frac{2\,\mu_0 n_1 n_2 iA'}{NA} \times \frac{\theta}{\theta'}$$

Hence magnetic induction B can be calculated, θ is maximum for particular orientation of the coil when the coil was perpendicular to the direction of field.

10.4.2. Hall Effect:

When a thin slice of rectangular semiconducting material such as gallium arsenide (GaAs), indium arsenide (InAs) or indium antimonide (InSb) through which a continuous current flows, placed in a magnetic field, then the magnetic flux lines exert a force on the semiconducting material which deflects the charge carriers, electrons and holes, to either side of the semiconducting strip (The arrangement is shown in following figure).

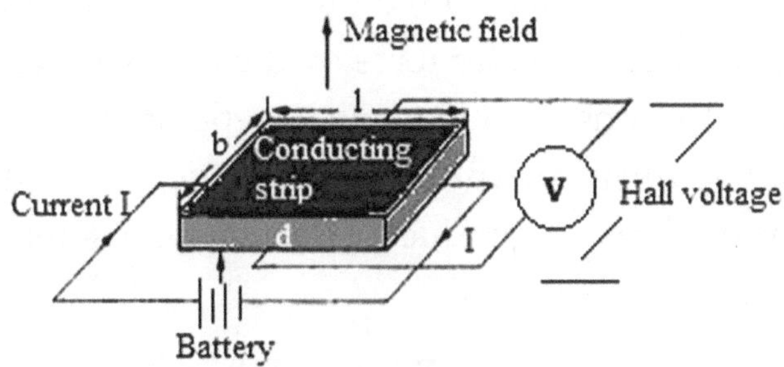

Figure: Hall Effect

This movement of charge carriers is a result of the magnetic force they experience passing through the semiconducting material. As these electrons and holes move a potential difference is produced between both sides of the semiconducting material by the build-up of these charge carriers. Then the movement of electrons through the semiconducting material is affected by the presence of an external magnetic field which is at right angles to it and this effect is greater in a flat rectangular shaped material. The effect of generating a measurable voltage by using a magnetic field is called the Hall Effect. The effect was discovered by E.H. Hall in 1879. The Hall Effect provides information regarding the type of magnetic pole and magnitude of the magnetic field.

The conductivity measurements cannot expose whether one or types of carriers neither are present nor distinguish between them. However, this information can be obtained from Hall Effect measurements, which are basic tools for the determination of mobilities.

A static magnetic field has no effect on charges unless they are in motion. When the charges flow, a magnetic field directed perpendicular to the direction of flow produces a mutually perpendicular force on the charges. When this happens, electrons and holes will be separated by opposite forces. They will in turn produce an electric field (Eh) which depends on the cross product of the magnetic intensity, H, and the current density, J.

$$Eh = R\ J \times H, \qquad \text{here R is the Hall coefficient.}$$

Consider a strip of semiconductor, the dimension of which are x, y and z. If J is directed along X-axis and H along Z-axis then Eh will be along Y-axis, then we can write,

$$R = [Vh/y]/\ JH = Vh.Z/\ I\ H$$

Where Vh is the Hall voltage appearing between the two surfaces perpendicular to y and I =J yz

To calculate the Hall voltage, assumed that all the carriers have the same drift velocity. If the carriers are of only one type for example, metals and doped semiconductors then, the magnetic force on the carriers is Em = e (v × H), where v is the drift velocity of the carriers.

We know that the current density 'J' is the product of charge q and the number of carriers traversing unit area in unit time, which is equivalent to the carrier density multiplied by the drift velocity.

i.e. J = q n v

By putting these values in above equation we get,

$$R = [Eh/JH] = [v.H/ q n v H] = 1/ n q$$

From this equation, it is clear that the sign of Hall coefficient depend upon the sign of the q. This means, in a p-type specimen the R would be positive, while in n type it would be negative. Also for a fixed magnetic field and input current, the Hall voltage is proportional to $1/n$ or its resistivity.

The conductivity of the material is $\sigma = nq\mu$.

Where 'μ' is the mobility of the charge carriers.

Thus $\mu = R\sigma$

This equation provides an experimental measurement of mobility. [6, 7, 8]

10.4.3. Measurement of flux density using Hall Effect:

The experimental setup requires:

1. Hall Effect Set-up

2. Electromagnet

3. Constant Current Power Supply

4. Hall Probe and

5. Digital Gaussmeter

The experimental set-up (as shown in following figure) of Hall Effect experiment consists of semiconductor strip of rectangular shape, total setup of two electromagnets with particular gap between the pole pieces, an electronic digital milivoltmeter and a constant current power supply. The Hall Voltage and probe current can be read on the same digital panel meter through the selector switch.

The Hall probe generally made up of Indium Arsenide crystal of rectangular shape. The crystal is covered by a protective layer of paint. The total system is mounted in a pen type case for further protection.

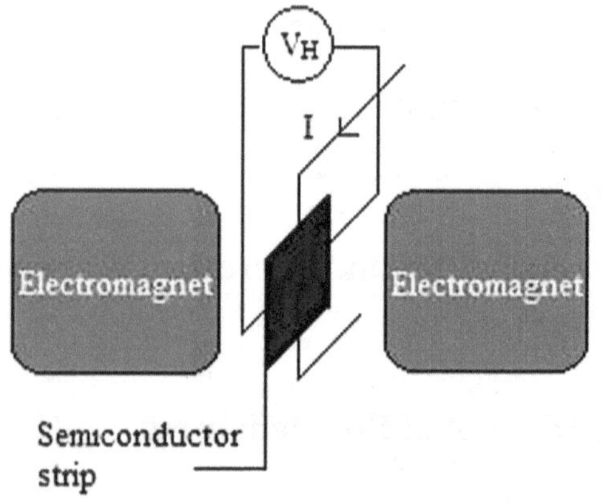

Figure : Experimetal setup of measureent
of magnetic field using Hall effect

The Gaussmeter operates on the principle of Hall Effect in semiconductors. A semiconductor material carrying current develops an electro-motive force, when placed in a magnetic field, in a direction perpendicular to the direction of both electric current and magnetic field. The magnitude of this EMF is proportional to the field intensity if the current is kept constant and this EMF is called as the Hall Voltage.

Experimental procedure:

1. Connect the widthwise contacts of the Hall Probe to the terminals marked 'Voltage' and lengthwise contacts to terminals marked 'Current'.

2. Switch 'ON' the Hall Effect set-up and adjustment current to some desired value, say few mA.

3. Switch over the display to voltage side. There may be some voltage reading even outside the magnetic field. This is due to imperfect alignment of the four contacts of the Hall Probe and is generally known as the 'Zero field Potential'.

4. Now place the probe in the magnetic field as shown in figure and switch on the electromagnet power supply and adjust the current to any desired value. When Hall probe will be perfectly perpendicular to magnetic field, the Hall voltage will be maximum.

5. Measure the Hall voltage for the direction of the current as well as for the magnetic field. Repeat for the different values of current and also of the magnetic fields.

6. Keeping the magnetic field constant, measure the Hall voltage as a function of current.

7. Measure the Hall voltage as a function of magnetic field keeping a suitable value of current as constant.

8. Measure the magnetic field by the Gaussmeter.

From the graph Hall voltage versus magnetic field calculate the Hall coefficient.

Also determine the type of majority charge carriers, i.e. whether the crystal is n type or type.

Calculate charge carrier density from the relation

$$R = 1/ n q$$

$$i.e. \ n = 1/ R q$$

Calculate carrier mobility, using the formula $\mu = R\sigma$. [8]

References

1. http://hyperphysics.phy-astr.gsu.edu/hbase/solids/magpr.htm.

2. www.school-for-champions.com/science/magnetic_materials.

3. http://www.electrical4u.com/questions-and-answers-on-magnetic-materials/

4. http://jittdl.physics.iupui.edu/jitt/sampler/physics/physics_archive/magneticmaterials.

5. http://what-when-how.com/materialsparts-and-finishes/magnetic-materials.

6. http://hyperphysics.phy-astr.gsu.edu/hbase/magnetic/hall.html.

7. www.schoolphysics.co.uk/age16-19/Electricity and magnetism/ Electromagnetism /text/ Measurement_of_magnetic_fields.

8. http://my.execpc.com/~rhoadley/magmetr1.htm.

9. User manual hall effect setup,www.sestechno.com

10. http://www.tutorhelpdesk.com/homeworkhelp/ Electricity-Magnetism-/Search-Coil-Method- Assignment-Help.html (Search coil)

Bibliography

1. Transducers and Instrumentation: D.V.S.Murthy.

2. Instrumentation: Devices and system: C.S.Rangan, G.R.Sharma, V.S.V.Mani.

3. Principles of measurement and Instrumentation: Alan S.Morris.

4. Electronic Instrumentation: H.S.Kalsi.

5. Electrical and electronic measurement Instrumentation: A.K.Sawhney.

6. Modern electronic instrumentation and measurement Technique: Helfrick Cooper.

7. Instrumentation: Measurement and analysis - Nakra and Chaudhary.

8. Electronic Measurement- U.A. Bakshi.

9. Electronic Instrumentation and measurement techniques, David Cooper and Heffrick.

10. Electrical and electronic measurements and Instrumentation, A.K. Sawhney.

11. Electricity and magnetism: D.C.Tayal.

12. Electricity and magnetism: Khare and Shrivastav.